Building a Joyful Life with Your Child who has Special Needs

Nancy J. Whiteman and Linda Roan-Yager

Jessica Kingsley Publishers
London and Philadelphia

Extracts on pp. 25 and 27 from *Let Your Life Speak: Listening for the Voice of Vocation* by Parker J. Palmer reproduced with permission of John Wiley & Sons, Inc.

First published in 2007
by Jessica Kingsley Publishers
116 Pentonville Road
London N1 9JB, UK
and
400 Market Street, Suite 400
Philadelphia, PA 19106, USA

www.jkp.com

Library of Congress Cataloging in Publication Data
A CIP catalog record for this book is available from the Library of Congress

British Library Cataloguing in Publication Data
A CIP catalogue record for this book is available from the British Library

ISBN-13: 978 1 84310 841 2
ISBN-10: 1 84310 841 0

Printed and bound in Great Britain by
Athenaeum Press, Gateshead, Tyne and Wear

Building a Joyful Life with Your Child who has Special Needs

Contents

Acknowledgements

Our sincere thanks to the parents for their candor and the wisdom they shared during our interviews, workshops, and coaching sessions. We learned so much from listening to your stories and insights.

Our own families, of course, have been our greatest teachers. Thank you for your understanding and patience while this book was being written.

Our friend and colleague Beret Strong provided tremendous guidance and tact in helping us shape and edit our thoughts into a book. Many thanks for all your help.

A Note on the Text

The names and identifying characteristics of the families in this book have been changed to respect their privacy.

While it is our hope that this book will be helpful to all readers, we recommend that anyone experiencing significant feelings of depression and anxiety also consult with a trusted medical professional and/or therapist.

About the Authors

Nancy Whiteman is the mother of two daughters. She holds a BS in Human Development from Cornell University and an MBA from the University of Massachusetts at Amherst. Nancy lives with her family in Boulder, Colorado.

Linda Roan-Yager has three daughters. Her oldest daughter was born with Down syndrome and cleft lip and palate. Besides mothering, Linda has over 15 years' experience supporting and challenging individuals in their own life journey and providing workshops that inspire. Linda holds an MA in School Psychology from Trinity University and a BA from Texas State University.

Nancy and Linda welcome feedback through their website www.shiftingview.com. Shifting View provides workshops, coaching and consulting for parents with children who have special needs as well as educators and other professionals that work with these families.

Introduction

Welcome to *Building a Joyful Life*. We are Nancy Whiteman and Linda Roan-Yager, the authors of this book. Before you dive into the content of this book, we'd like to tell you a little bit about this book and why it exists. *Building a Joyful Life* is truly a labor of love – the very personal outgrowth of our own experiences as two mothers of children with special needs.

Between our two daughters, we have experienced a range of special needs – from mental health and cognitive difficulties to developmental and physical disabilities. We did not meet one another until our children were 9 and 7 respectively. Soon after meeting, however, we found ourselves off in corners at parties, talking about our children but mostly talking about ourselves and our reactions to our children's situations. We were both intrigued to find that although our children had completely different challenges, our reactions and emotions were very similar.

Like many parents in our situation, we both immersed ourselves in information. If we were going to have children with special needs, then we were going to be experts on those needs! We avidly sought out books and other sources of information about our children's specific challenges so that we would be knowledgeable about their needs, appropriate interventions, and treatments.

As our knowledge on our children's needs grew, however, we found that our own issues came to the forefront. For both of us, life had become pretty grim. We had become consumed with our children's needs and had sorely neglected our own. Our lives lacked balance and we often felt depressed and anxious.

We followed somewhat different paths in our efforts to regain our equilibrium – we will share our own journey throughout the book. But both of us turned to books for inspiration and assistance in creating our ideal lives despite the challenges of raising our children.

Like Goldilocks, however, we just couldn't seem to find a book that "fit". Some were too hard (more academic and research-oriented than we wanted) while others were too soft (anecdotal or "personal story" books). While many books in the personal story genre chronicled parents' evolution from grief to joy, they never seemed to capture *how* these parents had made this important transition. The general "self-help" category offered many wonderful books on achieving balanced lives and joy but none that truly spoke to our unique challenges as parents of children with significant differences.

We eventually concluded that the book we were looking for did not exist and decided that *we* would write the book we wanted. Our objective was to write a book that would both comfort and inspire. It would not only share *our* stories, it would also help our readers transform their own stories. We wanted parents to finish our book and be filled with energy, excitement, and resolve to create full and joyful lives for themselves and their children.

But where to start? We knew that the answers would come from the parents themselves. Our first step was to interview parents about their own stories. As we listened, we began to notice consistent themes in the interviews of parents who were especially resilient and positive about their lives. These themes included the ability to build effective support systems for themselves and their children, to see their child as a whole person beyond his or her diagnosis, and to find personal meaning in their experiences. We organized the book around eight central themes that emerged from those discussions.

Merely sharing parent stories, no matter how wonderful, was not enough. We scrutinized each of these eight characteristics and asked ourselves, "What can we do to help our readers develop these qualities in themselves? What skills, information, or practice could be helpful to parents as each seeks a path to a joyful life?" This led to the development of exercises and tools which we "field tested" in our parent workshops. We populated each chapter with an array of exercises to help parents explore and, in some instances, shift their attitudes, beliefs, and behaviors to develop and strengthen qualities of resilience in themselves.

This book represents a deeply personal journey for us. It has given us the chance to step back from our own lives and challenges to reflect on where we have been, where we are today, and where we want to go. Talking with other parents and learning from their wisdom has been a healing and inspiring experience for us. Our goal in writing this book has been to distill that wisdom and make it accessible to other parents who face the same challenges.

Nancy:
If anyone had ever told me eight years that I would be writing a book about my child, her mental health, and the impact that it has had on my life, I would have been incredulous. At the time, my

daughter was a glorious, though intense, 2½-year-old. Verbally precocious, she began talking in full sentences by the time she was a year old and was actively debating the finer points of Winnie the Pooh with me by 18 months. At pre-school, other children flocked to her, enjoying her sense of humor, enthusiasm, and incredible imagination.

My husband John and I were delighted but not particularly surprised. After all, we were great parents, weren't we? We read to her, encouraged her, played with her, and adored her completely. I wasn't naïve enough to expect totally smooth sailing but, like many people, I'd built my life around the assumption that life was going to be, if not perfect, at least imperfect in the usual relatively minor and predictable ways. I was prepared for the idea that my kids wouldn't be angels. I anticipated a few challenging adolescent years with angst and rebellion. Unappealing as I found it, I could even imagine a certain amount of body piercing in locations other than ear lobes. But a child with a mental illness was simply not part of my consciousness. Things like that just didn't happen to me.

Then I found out that things like this *did* happen to me. My beloved daughter began having severe behavior problems just before the age of four. While she had always been an intense child, she became irritable, explosive, and inflexible. A juice glass out of place or a parental "no" could trigger a 40-minute rage. Friends became wary as she attempted to orchestrate every aspect of their play and blew up at them with the slightest provocation. At pre-school, her teachers noted that she seemed unable to follow simple two-step directions and would sometimes wander aimlessly around the room. She began to have trouble sleeping and talked incessantly as if her thoughts were racing.

At first we attributed her behavior to the recent arrival of her little sister, but when her moods persisted for months, we began to get more and more concerned. John and I began to make the rounds of professionals trying to figure out what had suddenly gone so wrong. After trying occupational therapy, behavioral therapy, and holistic and nutritional treatments (we live in Boulder, Colorado – holistic center of the universe – after all!), we finally consulted a psychiatrist, and at age 5½, she was diagnosed with early onset bipolar disorder and started on medication.

I was devastated. In addition to my overwhelming concern about Kirsten, I also worried about myself and my life. What did this mean for our family? What would the future hold? How would I manage a career with a child who required so much care?

And underneath these concerns were even more personal (and more embarrassing) worries. What would other people think? I had always taken a certain amount of comfort in the thought that I could manage people's perceptions of me. I wanted the world to see me as competent, successful, happy, and together. Part of this image, in my mind, was to have bright, well-behaved, and well-adjusted children. But, as Kirsten's illness progressed, maintaining an ideal image became impossible. Friends and strangers alike witnessed Kirsten's public rages and our often inept handling of them. I couldn't protect myself from the well-meaning advice of family and friends who offered their ideas on how to improve her behavior or the disgusted looks from strangers who would *never* allow their children to behave so badly. I silently suffered and fumed as people who knew next to nothing about childhood bipolar assured me that it was the new "trendy" diagnosis and wondered if we had simply considered changing her diet or if we were afraid to discipline her.

For the next three years, my feelings see-sawed between despair, denial, and brief periods of resolving to be "positive" and hopeful (which, not surprisingly, usually coincided with Kirsten's periods of stability). John and I spent the majority of our time together discussing Kirsten and what we should do next. Our lives were completely dominated by Kirsten's needs; they were all consuming. And barely under the surface of my concern for Kirsten, my own depression and rage was building. Our social life dwindled as getting together with "normal" families became too stressful and painful. Instead of sharing the wonderful family adventures we had anticipated, we hunkered down at home, watching videos with the kids and waiting for the next shoe to drop, the next mood to shift, the next rage to strike. Kirsten struggled academically and my own anxiety about her academic performance and social adjustment was so severe that I got a stomach ache almost every time I walked through the doors of her classroom.

Finally, when Kirsten was 6½, we hit on a combination of medications that seemed to do the trick. For a few joyous months, we had our happy little girl back again. Even with the undesirable side effects, it was worth it to see her smiling and relaxed again. Her charismatic ability to instantly make friends was back. We were overjoyed and scheduled our first ever family vacation, renting a cottage in Maine and making plans to spend a few weeks visiting family and friends all over New England.

Three days after arriving in Boston, however, Kirsten had a complete medication failure and was back to ground zero. It was a miserable trip (John and I agreed not to refer to the experience as a "vacation") and we came home depressed and exhausted. Back home, things did not improve despite more medication changes. We were back to the "bad old days" as we called them.

For me, this relapse was more difficult than anything I had experienced to date. It was then that I realized how much I had been hoping that we would find the magic cure – the right "cocktail" of medications – and our lives could all go back to what we had expected on the basis of her sunny early childhood. But, along with the medication failure, came a dose of reality: this illness was real; it was serious and it was probably forever.

My grief was intense as I tried to integrate this new perspective: it wasn't going to be all right. I was really going to have to figure out how to live with this. I felt overwhelmed, furious, and depleted. At John's urging, I decided to see a therapist myself.

At our first meeting, she asked me what had brought me to see her. I launched into a 40-minute recitation of Kirsten, her history, her problems, and my grief. At the end of my monologue, she said to me, "Now I know something about your daughter but I still don't know much about you." I stared at her. Frankly, I was stunned. Hadn't I just told the woman everything important that there was to know about me? What more was there to say? What did she want from me?

In retrospect, however, I can see that this conversation was a turning point for me. Her reaction made it clear to me how much *I* had gone away. There seemed to be very little *me* left. My feelings and moods had more or less become interwoven with Kirsten's; when she was doing well, I was doing well. When she was having a rough time, so was I.

Once I realized how much I had allowed my own life to be diminished by Kirsten's illness, I began to work on my attitudes and the perceptions. With my therapist's help, I started to see how my laser focus on Kirsten's situation was not serving either her or me. No matter how hard I tried, no matter how much I read and how expert I became, I couldn't "make" her better. There were practical things we could and did do, but this was one problem that wasn't going to yield to a "can do" attitude.

At the suggestion of my therapist, I began a journal, something I had done consistently after Kirsten became ill, but then abandoned. I found, however, that journaling was not what I needed at that time. I was bored and impatient with my own musings and quickly became tired of exploring the same themes over and over without feeling like I was moving towards any sort of resolution.

"How do other people survive this?", I wondered. I prowled the stacks at the library and the self-help and special needs sections of book stores. I found a number of great books on children with mental illnesses and other special needs. But, to my dismay, I found that the vast majority of these books focused on helping the child but had relatively little to say on what the experience was like for the parents. The books that were focused on the parental experience were often of the personal story genre featuring parents who had successfully moved beyond their grief and anger to acceptance and joy. They were all inspiring and uplifting stories but they never seemed to talk about *how* they made that all important transition. It just seemed to happen with time.

I wanted to know the secret. What did these parents know or do that I did not? The answer, I decided, was to be found in talking with other parents who were further along the path than I.

That is how the germ of the idea that ultimately became this book took root. I became interested in writing a book that would help me, as well as others, understand how other parents had successfully made this transition. I wanted to know how they found the inner strengths and energy to make their lives full, joyous, and even enviable despite the real challenges and limitations imposed by their children's situations.

The first person I approached for an interview was my friend and now business partner Linda Roan-Yager. As I expected, Linda had incredible insights and wisdom about her experiences in parenting her lovely daughter Miah. Our conversation led to a professional collaboration in this book and as well as a series of workshops and coaching offerings.

As we both began to interview parents with children with differences, we began to hear certain themes emerging fairly consistently from the parents who described themselves as living full and joyful lives. We decided to organize the book around those themes. To address the "how did they do it" aspect into the book, we decided to develop and include specific exercises designed to help parents develop those characteristics in themselves. We like to say that we tried to write the book that we wished we had found when we were newly dealing with our feelings about our children's situations.

This book represents a deeply personal journey for us. It has given us the chance to step back from our own lives and challenges to reflect on where we have been, where we are today and where we want to go. Talking with other parents and learning from their wisdom has been a healing and inspiring experience for us. Our goal in this book has been to distill that wisdom and make it accessible to other parents who face the same challenges. It is our hope that reading this book and completing the exercises within it will support you on your own path to a joyful and fulfilling life.

Linda:

My first pregnancy was a truly blissful time. I remember daydreaming daily about my much awaited beautiful baby. What would she look like, what kind of person would she become? I had no prenatal tests other than the standard ones and everything seemed to tick along just fine until my third trimester. This once extremely active baby just seemed to quit moving. I went to the obstetrician who immediately sent me to the hospital for tests. A high resolution ultrasound was done and I remember the technician saying, "At least the baby doesn't have Down syndrome. The head isn't flat in the back." I remember thinking, "What in the world is he talking about? There's no way this baby has anything seriously wrong. It's been so active. I've taken such good care of myself…"

When Miah was born a few weeks later after an easy, dreamlike birth, the pediatrician suggested we do some genetic testing. Why? True, our beautiful little girl was having trouble eating but that was understandable since she was born with a cleft lip and submucousal cleft palate. But the nurses kept covering her mouth and staring at her eyes. After days of pure agony waiting for the test results, the pediatrician gave us the news: Miah had Down syndrome. I remember getting a milkshake with my husband and sister on the drive home. At least we knew. And we had *known* for days anyway.

What followed was five years of looking like I was living life with strength and purpose... But really I was dying on the inside. My whole interior life revolved around my daughter's disability. I remember one day in the first few weeks of her life, ripping all the linens out of the closet as I cried and screamed. This seemed so unfair to me, but mostly, so unfair to Miah. I later remember wondering if I'd ever think about anything else. I looked like I was functioning fine. In fact, some service providers coined the term, "Ivy League parent" to describe how well I and some other parents in the disability center's playgroup helped their kids. It was true. I did everything possible to help Miah. But at the cost of my own mental health.

One perceptive service provider noticed my grief and helped me more than she will ever know. She already saw my child as a whole, complete, perfect human being and wanted me to feel that same hope for her that she did! Instead of suggesting a play strategy for my daughter she asked if *I'd* like to see a therapist – someone who spoke to a lot of parents in my position. I did – thank God! – And the next year I embarked on a personal journey of exploring my own beliefs about differences, my fears, and worked hard at creating personal meaning about my situation – all factors explored in this book. I felt better!

When my third daughter was born, however, almost six years after Miah's birth, I hit rock bottom again. The demands of three children, raging post pregnancy hormones, and pain I felt in not having a *big girl* pushed me to my breaking point. I felt so angry at Miah for not being able to do the things other 6-year-olds did with a new baby and a 2-year-old under foot. I felt like Linda Blair in *The Exorcist* with my head spinning around on my body some moments. And then a miracle happened. I remembered the first words I spoke to Miah as she lay on my tummy right after she was born. "You will have a wonderful life." And she did. She danced, played, and loved life... However, I had not made that same promise to myself, and it showed. It was time. This moment, the act of setting the intention – I would be happy, *I would not let this situation consume me, and I would have a great life too!* – became such a beacon of hope for me. I became *curious.* What did other people do that had been through something they found particularly hard, life-altering? I read, and read, and read, self-help book after self-help book. And I wrote, and wrote, and wrote, journal after journal. I took time for myself – a cup of tea, some quiet reflection, hikes and dancing. And I talked, and talked, and talked to my friends Beret and Catherine, my dance group, and I even hired a life coach to challenge my perceptions. Yes, two other cornerstones of this book – self-care and finding my own support network – were instrumental for me. And after awhile, guess what, it worked. I felt so much better, lighter, and more joyful. My thoughts about disability, my daughter, and my life changed. I realized that Miah's and my situations were hard, but exaggerated by my fear and tension, plus the belief that things would *always* be hard for her and me. Not by time itself, but by intention, working with my own thoughts (reframing, another tool taught in this book), and practice with the support of others, I began to heal. And working on this book has only strengthened my conviction that we can affect our future, our outlook for our child's life and our own by first wanting to do so and then committing not to stop until life feels more joyful.

For me, identifying how to make life *sweeter* made all the difference. Being grateful, laughing, noticing joy, softening and accepting my situation, practicing releasing my worries, trusting Miah and trusting Spirit all make life so much happier. I had to remember who I am, notice the good, slow down, and relax in order to find the peace I was craving. This book will give you tools to accomplish this.

For me, the biggest healing came from realizing my ruminations were getting me nowhere, and for that matter, were getting Miah nowhere either, *fast*. I started replacing my negativity with thoughts like: "Teach her happiness and love are within." And, "it's not what you do; it's who you are that I love." These thoughts seem so much more compassionate, centered, and strong – qualities I hold dear. This book will help you identify your own musings, thus, we believe, giving you a sense of centeredness and hope. I also began noticing my judgments about others and myself turning towards compassion. By taking time to withdraw from the pressures of the day, creating a little space for myself so I could fully engage my heart and mind to consider my own issues and life, I began to ponder a different path for myself and a different way to mother – less worry and more enjoying. I am happier and more trusting of Miah and her abilities now. Her situation (her speech problems, the way the world reacts to her, and how hard some things are for her) can still push my buttons, which only tells me there is still more work to do. But something is profoundly different now – I am able to *move on* more quickly to enjoy the life that is waiting for me. By practicing the principles of this book, and finally living them as much of the time as I can, I feel so much more relaxed, centered, and happy. And I know you will too.

We chose a workbook approach for this book because we feel it is imperative to *do the work*. It is one thing to understand something intellectually, and quite another for it to register emotionally. By actually engaging with the exercises you will come in contact with your own story. We encourage you to do this work slowly. Give yourself time for the ah-ha's to appear. And don't try to do this work when others are demanding your time. Make this your time. Treat it as a retreat — some private time carved out of your busy week. What about creating a sacred space with soft music and candlelight if this feels soothing to you? And also be gentle with yourself. If deep feelings surface that seem overwhelming, know that you have hit on something profoundly important. You may need to find outside help to process your emotions. Finding a good therapist to talk with might be the biggest gift you can give yourself and your child.

If your child has been diagnosed recently you might flip through this book and then put it on your shelf for a while, knowing that adjustment takes time and working on your own issues needs to happen when you are feeling safe and grounded enough to explore them. It is our experience that this is best done when one has moved past the early shock of diagnosis.

We hope time with this book is a creative journey that produces healing and joy.

CHAPTER 1

Springing Back and Moving Forward: Resilience and Happiness

The happiness of your life depends upon the quality of your thoughts.

Marcus Aurelius, Roman emperor, circa 278–312CE

We began this book with a sense of genuine curiosity about what makes some people able to thrive while many others struggle. Do they employ particular conscious tools and techniques, is it inborn temperament, situational, or a combination of many things?

When interviewing parents who were clearly living a joyful life with their children with special needs, it became clear that these parents were unusually resilient – that is, they had qualities that gave them far better odds for achieving a joyful life despite the challenges they faced in parenting their children.

This led us to think about what it actually means to be resilient and how people become that way. We also wanted to understand how resiliency contributes to happiness. As we dug in, we were fascinated to find an entire body of research and literature devoted to the study of resilience and happiness. Our reading in these areas was invaluable in helping us to see these remarkable parents in a broader context and to develop a framework for helping parents think about their own attitudes and behaviors. In this chapter, we want to share a few of the frameworks that provided a helpful lens to us as we listened to parents and tried to distill their elusive recipe for happiness.

What is resilience?

Resilience refers to the ability to survive and even thrive in the face of difficult circumstances and situations.

One of the clearest and most concise explanations of resiliency we found came from a group called International Resilience Project, a three-year pilot program funded by the Canadian government. This project looks at the individual, interpersonal, family, community, and cultural factors associated with resilience among youths aged 12–19 (Ungar 2005).

The project found that resilience consisted of seven distinct clusters of strength that are mobilized when we face difficult times. We found these characteristics fascinating as they mapped very closely with many of the qualities that we observed in the parents we interviewed. These seven clusters included:

Insight

Insight is the ability to ask tough questions and give honest answers. In adults, insight takes the form of *understanding*, which includes empathy, comprehension of the self and others, and a tolerance for complexity and ambiguity.

Raising a child with a disability or illness is fraught with complex feelings, conflicting and shifting emotions, and ambiguous outcomes. It calls on us not only to have empathy for our child but for everyone who is impacted by the situation – especially ourselves! It also takes tremendous courage to ask and hear the answers to the tough questions that arise around our children's situation.

Independence

In the parlance of the project, independence referred to the ability to distance oneself emotionally and physically from the source of pain. In its less mature forms, independence often manifested itself as emotional disengagement.

While emotional disengagement can be a healthy strategy for some situations such as an abusive parent or a critical boss, in general the parents we interviewed were extremely emotionally engaged with their children. Their independence takes the form of what the project refers to as *"separating"* – taking control over the power of their pain – including the ability to acknowledge and examine their pain without letting it control and dominate their lives. The reframing work outlined in Chapter 4 is particularly helpful in allowing people to step back from their painful feelings and develop alternative ways of viewing their situation.

Relationships

Clearly the ability to develop meaningful connections to other people is an essential component of mental health for all people. Our resilient parents, whether married or unmarried, shared the ability to find people who supported them and whom they supported. They were able to build close relationships that sustained and validated them and their children. We look at this quality in depth in Chapters 6 and 7 on building our children's community and building our own support network.

Initiative

Initiative is the ability to take charge of problems in a proactive way. The project referred to the adult version of initiative as *generating*, which they describe as "a zest for projects and for tackling challenging situations."

While many parents we interviewed would admit that their lives are too hectic to have much of a zest for starting new projects, it was clear that these parents shared a talent for tackling challenging situations. Time and time again, we were impressed by the problem-solving skills the parents displayed as well as the sheer persistence they exhibited in advocating for their children. As one mother noted, "Just because you lose one battle doesn't mean that you don't get in there again for the next fight."

Creativity and humor

The project sees these two strengths are related. Creativity involves using imagination and expressing oneself in art forms while humor is described as finding the comic in the tragic.

A number of parents we interviewed used some type of art form – painting, dancing, or collage – to explore and express their feelings through creativity. Virtually all parents we spoke with who were thriving agreed that humor was an essential component to getting through the daily challenges they face.

Morality

The last factor, morality, was described as acting on the basis of an informed conscience. In its adult manifestation, morality takes the form of *serving* – a sense of obligation to contribute to the well being of others.

That certainly resonated for us based on our interviews. We were struck by the generosity of spirit of these parents who, despite continual and often exhausting demands on their own time and resources, managed to be actively involved in support work and advocacy. Chapter 8 looks at the many amazing ways resilient parents have transformed their situations into conscious action in the world.

Survivor's personality

We found another helpful framework in the book *The Survivor Personality* by Al Siebert (1996). In this book, he describes the characteristics of people with survivor personalities as follows:

- they have survived a major crisis or challenge
- they have surmounted the crisis through personal effort
- they have emerged from the experience with previously unknown strengths and abilities, and
- they are able to find value in the experience.

We were struck by how well these characteristics described the families we interviewed. A universal characteristic of our "survivors" was that they emerged from their initial devastation over their child's condition stronger, more confident, and astonishingly positive. Our job in writing this book was to understand how that transition happened.

Finally, our work was strongly influenced by the work of another team of researchers, Rick Foster and Greg Hicks. These two men set off on an ambitious project to understand what makes some people happier than others. They developed a rigorous screening process to identify people who fit their criteria for happiness and ultimately interviewed hundreds of people. Their objective was to look beyond the usual temperamental attributes that we associate with happy people and to understand how the specific attitudes and choices these people made resulted in their feelings of well being. The result was a book entitled *How We Choose to be Happy: The Nine Choices of Extremely Happy People* (2004).

The authors identified nine sets of choices that happy people make which contribute to their high level of personal satisfaction and well being.

1. Intention: happy people are conscious of their desire to be happy. They recognize that having a happy life is an objective and are willing to work towards it.

2. Accountability: happy people see themselves as being responsible for their own happiness.

3. Identification: happy people know what make them happy; they are clear on their own needs and desires.

4. Centralizing: happy people organize their lives around the things that give them joy. They make choices that support their needs.

5. Recasting: happy people are able to reframe painful experiences by looking at them through a new and more positive lens.

6. Options: happy people see themselves as having choices.

7. Appreciation: happy people recognize and appreciate the good things in their lives.

8. Giving: happy people find giving back to others to be an important aspect of their own happiness.

9. Synergy: the various parts of happy people's lives reinforce their choices towards happiness.

We found a great deal of overlap between Foster and Hicks' set of choices and what we heard from the resilient parents that we interviewed. The challenge for us was in seeing how these types of choices played themselves out in the context of the serious and ongoing demands of parenting children with exceptional needs. Could parents with a child with serious medical needs, for example, truly centralize their lives around what they loved to do? How did the idea of having options translate to a family whose life was organized around meeting the needs of their schizophrenic child? In other words, we wondered if these principles, which made sense in theory, could actually be applied in chronic, stressful parenting situations.

How this book is organized

While these models were enormously helpful, we have found that parenting a child with special needs creates its own unique challenge which calls on us to put these characteristics of resilience, happiness, and survival to work in very specific and unique ways.

As we interviewed parents, we began to identify a specific set of characteristics that the resilient parents we interviewed seemed to share. Consequently, the book explores each of these seven characteristics in depth in the following chapters. For each of these characteristics, we provide some anecdotes from our interviews as well as a set of exercises that reinforce the characteristics.

Specifically, the book examines the following qualities:

1. a belief in the intention to lead a joyful life and the importance of self-care

2. the ability to accept and embrace complex, ambiguous, and ever changing feelings about our child's situation

3. the ability to reframe negative thoughts

4. being able to see beyond our children's diagnosis

5. building our child's community

6. building our own support systems

7. finding personal meaning in the experience of parenting our children with differences.

While the book's chapters were sequenced to build on one another, you may find it helpful to read the chapters "out of order" if there is a topic that speaks to a particular issue or need you are facing at this time.

CHAPTER 2

Putting on Your Oxygen Mask:
Intention and Self-care

Self-care is never a selfish act – it is simply good
stewardship of the only gift I have, the gift I was
put on earth to offer to others. Anytime we can
listen to our true self, and give it the care it requires,
we do so not only for ourselves, but for the many
others whose lives we touch.

Parker J. Palmer (1999, p.30)

Nancy:

I spend a lot of time on airplanes and I have to confess that I
generally ignore the flight attendants' request to pay attention while
they review the latest safety features of the plane. But even as I am
reading my magazine or finishing up one last game of Hearts before
being told to turn off my computer, one thing always seems to break
through my inattention. "In the event of an emergency, oxygen
masks will automatically drop down from the overhead compart-
ment. Please adjust your own oxygen mask first before assisting a
child." It seems at once obvious and profound. I think of myself on a
plummeting plane with my two beloved girls. There is no doubt in
my mind that my first panicked response would be to try to ensure
their safety. Yet I can also clearly picture myself fumbling around
with their oxygen masks while they flail around (and complain that
the elastic strap is bothering them!). I could easily pass out from lack
of oxygen before I ever get them settled and safe. So, I always
appreciate the little reminder to take care of myself first before
tending to their needs.

Why is this lesson so hard for me to apply to my life on the ground? Without the drama of an emergency, I find it all too easy to forget about my own needs and to focus on theirs. I know I'm not unique. Such is the nature of parenthood, and especially of parenthood when your child has an illness or disability. While a certain amount of self-sacrifice is part of parenting, I have found that I've needed to examine my own assumptions about how much is desirable and what I tell myself about my choices. My responses to the exercises in this chapter help me remember to focus on what I want my life to look like and how I can get there. I keep these responses where I can look at them regularly – they are my on-the-ground flight attendant reminding me that I'm no good to anyone else if I can't breathe myself.

Linda:

I recently worked with a very bright, active woman who relayed, with much anxiety and stress in her voice, a harrowing picture of evening hours at her house. She would rush to get a meal on the table while helping her kids with homework. Inevitably the kids would begin to fight and she would get increasingly stressed as the hours went on. She desperately wanted some time to herself after the kids were in bed, but that too was hard. Her marriage was suffering. She had resorted to drinking a couple of cocktails during this evening time to help her "cope."

We brainstormed about what she could do to relax and be more centered during this time, but she came up with nothing. The truth was that those evening hours *were* busy. The kids had to do their homework then because of after-school activities earlier in the day. Dinner had to be served. She had already implemented strategies to make dinner preparation easier.

What she came to, however, was that *she* could be different during this time. When she looked at her entire day, she realized that she never stopped. Even her exercise – undertaken for self-care – felt *busy*. She decided she needed to change what happened before the evening hours. If she took one hour during the day to sit, needlepoint, and *just be*, then she was calmer, happier, and more present during the evening, and so was everyone else. When I talked to her three weeks later, she reported no longer feeling the need for the cocktail because her self-care during the day carried her into the night.

In my own life, I have discovered that my stress level is less about the situation and more about my attitude. And my attitude is directly correlated with my own level of self-care. Have I taken time to write in my journal, am I making time for friends, what about dance class, is there *any fun* in my week?

In her book, *The Artist's Way* (1996), Julia Cameron encourages us to be kind to ourselves in small, concrete ways daily. She also encourages blocking out a couple of hours each week to nurture ourselves with fun and frivolity. How about doing one nice thing for yourself daily? How about a little solitude for yourself daily? How about checking in with yourself several times a day? Ask yourself, "How am I feeling?", and then respond to yourself kindly. If it feels like you will never be able to afford the time, identify that thought as resistance. If we really think about it, our lives are so busy and we are responsible for so much and so many important people (such as our children) that we need to take care of ourselves and be at our best. I know that I am way less effective when I am tired, harried, or depressed. So why is building in time for myself so hard? Julia Cameron says that it is not time or money that makes self-care difficult. It is the fear of intimacy – self-intimacy. What am I hiding from? Julia says that time for ourselves will acquaint us with who we are and what we want. This can feel scary, but it can fill our creative reserves and lead to a more fulfilling, joyful life. And that is definitely what I want.

The power of intention

Have you ever heard this joke? How many therapists does it take to change a light bulb? Answer: Only one, but the light bulb has to *really* want to change.

This may not be the funniest joke you've ever heard, but it is relevant to the key point of this chapter. We believe that the *desire* to see our lives change for the better is a prerequisite for that change to occur. Sure, we know that, once in a blue moon, someone will inherit a fortune from a long-lost relative or have their dream job land in their lap. But, for most of us, we must have intentions about how we want our lives to be before we can begin to make meaningful changes. This chapter is devoted to articulating our intentions for our ideal lives and developing the plans that will enable us to achieve them.

In *How We Choose to Be Happy* (2004), Rick Foster and Greg Hicks share the following insight about the role of intention in the happy people that they studied:

> Intention is the force behind all happiness... It's compelling because it initiates an adventure that's waiting to happen. It's the prelude of things to come... The intention to be happy is a mindset that propels us toward living as happily as we can, predisposing us to make each day as joyful and significant as it can be. It's the point at which we stop responding unconsciously and actively decide we want to be happy. We make a promise to ourselves, a commitment to happiness that becomes our compass, guiding the decisions we make and the actions we take. ...If we don't truly intend to make happiness a reality, we have unconsciously chosen something different. Without setting our intention, even fleeting happiness is haphazard. But once we have our intention firmly in place, happiness is no longer accidental, it is purposeful – something we are creating all day long. (p. 20)

Intention is the start of it all. In our workshops, we try to get a gauge on the level and type of intention in the room by asking everyone to introduce themselves and share something that they hope to get out of the day. This helps us understand our participants' needs and set expectations appropriately.

The most frequent responses are that parents are looking for ideas and support on achieving more balance in their lives and a sense of personal empowerment. As one mother put it, "I want some ideas on how I can feel more in control of my life and my time. Sometimes I feel like I'm on automatic pilot."

Life beyond being the good parent

Beyond the intention implicit in these responses we hear another important message – the belief that they deserve happier and fuller lives, that *they* matter enough to deserve the fruition of their own dreams and hopes.

That can be a difficult message for parents in the midst of their struggles to remember. We often get a sense of where parents are coming from when we ask them to share one objective they have for the day. While most people who attend our workshop understand that the workshop is focused on them, we always have a few parents who say that their objective for the day is to learn new strategies for helping their children or to become better parents to their children.

To these parents, we respond that while they may pick up some strategies for helping their children, the primary focus of the day will be on them and their own lives. And, while we wholeheartedly believe that having balance in one's life does promote effective parenting, the workshop focuses on building joyful lives because parents deserve wonderful lives, too – whether or not it benefits their children. Some people are visibly uncomfortable at that the thought of being asked to focus on their own needs for an entire day.

Why are so many of us inclined to put ourselves last? Why do we seem to value our own life goals less than our other responsibilities?

Part of the answer, we believe, is societal. In *Your Heart's Desire* (1997), Sonia Choquette, PhD., points out that seeing our own dreams as valuable can be difficult in our society. She calls it the "you must finish all your homework before you can go out and play" syndrome. It is an internalized parental voice telling us to get everything else done before attending to our own needs. The problem is our work is never done, so time to focus on ourselves never arrives. We may even feel morally superior to put others before ourselves, work excessively, or deny ourselves fun and pleasure.

But some of the answer is also situational. Our children have so many needs and those needs are often urgent and all consuming. For many of us, putting our children's needs first has become an ingrained habit that feels natural and comfortable, even if it's not completely satisfying. A free evening after the kids are in bed is spent researching the latest treatment options on the Internet. A dinner with our spouse is spent discussing the next round of medications and therapies. It is easy to see that after years of focusing on their needs, paying attention to our own needs feels like a selfish impulse.

Some parents even begin to define themselves primarily or solely around their children. We have noticed, for example, in many online support groups, that parents will select screen names such as "Ryansmom". Our own identity becomes subsumed in our children's identity. We almost forget how to talk to our spouse and our friends about other topics and areas of interest. Mother Teresa uses the analogy of needing to put oil in a lamp to keep it burning. It is the same with our relationships. Without regular attention and focused energy, they lose their vitality and meaning.

The cost of losing ourselves

What we may not realize is that this lack of balance ultimately carries a significant cost both to us and to the important relationships in our lives. Seligman and Darling, authors of *Ordinary Families, Special Children* (1997), have researched this question. They report that parents of children with differences often experience high levels of stress over long periods of time. This emotional stress may cause worry, fear, lack of sleep, and loss of energy. This type of chronic, high level stress can also be damaging to interpersonal relationships.

Research by Theresa Early and Thomas Gregoire (2002) at Ohio State University also looks at this issue and finds that parents caring for children with emotional disorders suffer an increasingly greater burden over time. The effect of the child's behavior on the parents intensifies and becomes more significant as time passes. In other words, most parents do *not* "get used to" caring for these children. Their situation takes an increasing toll on the family and on the psychological health of the children.

Not surprisingly, this research has also shown a connection between stress and interpersonal interactions in other types of relationships as well, such as interactions between parents and mental health staff. The research also found that parents who received problem-solving training on how to identify, recognize reactions to, and generate ideas to combat stressful situations, experienced less stress than the parents who did not receive this training.

By the time most parents reach our workshop, they have already figured out that what they are doing is not helping them lead a joyful life. Our job is to help them see a way out. Sometimes, though, years of putting their own needs last have taken their toll even in terms of being clear about *what* they want or how they can get there. They see no way to move towards the life they want. Many have even forgotten what it was that used to give them pleasure. Remembering this, in our experience, is the first step towards building a joyful life.

Exercise 2.1: Our basic needs

Healthy self-care starts with asking ourselves if we are meeting our basic needs. We define basic needs as essentials such as food, water, and sleep. These basic needs should be non-negotiable, but sometimes we are so busy that we neglect even the basics.

This list, adapted from Jennifer Louden's *The Woman's Comfort Book: A Self-Nurturing Guide for Restoring Balance in Your Life* (1992), will help you assess where you are now in terms of your self-care.

Check off the needs you are meeting regularly.

☐ Do you usually get 7–8 hours of sleep?

☐ Do you eat healthy food daily?

☐ Do you allow yourself time to be outside, no matter how briefly?

☐ Do you get enough sunlight, especially in the wintertime?

☐ Do you drink enough water?

☐ Do you see a doctor and dentist as often as you should?

Beyond the basics, we also have secondary needs. We could live without fulfilling these needs, but probably not with great joy. Check off the secondary needs that you are meeting regularly.

☐ Do you feel you get enough *fun* exercise?

☐ Do you make time for friendship?

☐ Do you have an outlet of release for your negative emotions?

☐ Do you do things that give you a sense of fulfillment and purpose?

☐ Do you make time for solitude?

☐ Are you getting spiritual nourishment?

☐ Can you remember the last time you had a good laugh?

Look back over the two lists and sum up how you feel you are doing in meeting your basic and secondary needs.

Exercise 2.2: Rediscovering what makes you feel joyful

Imagine that you are presented with the ultimate gift: three days with nothing to do. That's right, no responsibilities, no children, no work, no household chores, nothing. What's more, you are guaranteed that your children/spouse/job responsibilities and any other commitments will be flawlessly handled in your absence. There is absolutely nothing for you to worry about.

Let's do some fantasizing about what you would do with this gift of time.

1. Where would you go to spend your free time? Would you stay home or go somewhere else? Are you mostly planning on being inside or outside? (Don't let budget or distance constrain you – this is all paid for and you can get there and back instantly.)

2. You can bring anything you want with you – books, hobbies, music, people or anything else you would like. What or who do you want to bring?

3. How do you want to spend your time during your three days? What activities or experiences would you like to have?

4. What does this fantasy tell you about what you would like to have more of in your life?

The energy pie

Understanding where your energy is going today is also an important step in setting your intention about how you would like your life to change. The nineteenth-century American writer and philosopher Henry David Thoreau once wrote that "things don't change; we change". This next exercise is designed to help you think about where you would like to change.

If you think of your life as a big pie, this exercise encourages you look at the slices that represent different areas in your life and how much energy each is getting. We talk about "energy" versus "time" in this exercise, because we are mostly concerned with where your emotional energy is going. Our job, for example, may technically take up 30 percent of our day but if we spend a lot of our time at work worrying about our child, it may be getting significantly less than 30 percent of our mental energy.

Once we complete the current energy pie, we redo the pie with our "ideal" energy allocations.

Before you get started, we want to make a few comments about this exercise.

- There is nothing set in stone about the categories that we have selected, so feel free to modify them to fit your life and situation. If we have omitted a category that is important to you, highlight its importance by labeling it on your pie chart. Eliminate categories that don't work for you.

- Don't "over-think" your energy allocations. Precision doesn't matter. Just try to give each category an approximate percentage.

- Know that it is pretty common to rework your energy allocations a few times before you land on the percentages that you feel realistically represent your life.

  Nancy:
  When I first did this exercise myself, I thought that Kirsten received 85 percent of my energy. When I went to fill in the rest of my categories, I realized this couldn't possibly be true – even though it felt like it to me at the time! I ended up at around 55 percent but it took me a few tries to get there.

- Everyone defines their categories differently. Some people dump all their miscellaneous time-sucking activities into "other" while other people put activities that they valued highly into the "other" category. We suggest that you put things that are really important to you in a separate category.

- There is no good or bad in this exercise. Just because you are spending a lot of time in one area of your life doesn't necessarily mean that your life is out of balance. Your chart may represent exactly what you want to be doing right now. Or it may not. Only you know. The second half of the exercise helps you look objectively at whether your current energy allocations are right for you.

- Recognize that energy can be positive or negative. One person might assign 65 percent of her energy into a certain area of her life and feel wonderful about it, while another person might assign the same percentage to that area and feel miserable about it. Your percentages are far less important than how you feel about how you are expending your precious energy.

When you complete your ideal energy pie, don't get hung up on whether your ideal energy allocations are realistic. It's OK either way.

Remember, the purpose of this exercise is to articulate our intentions and work toward them. The chart is a visual representation of where your energy is going and where you want it to go. If you are already at your ideal allocations, that is wonderful. If not, the second part of the exercise provides a framework for thinking about where and how you might make changes.

Exercise 2.3: How I spend my energy today

The list of categories below represents various options for how we spend our energy. Think about the categories and allocate the percent of your energy that you feel you devote to each one. Think of this as your *emotional* energy rather than your actual *physical* energy. Refine these categories to fit your own life. Make sure the total adds up to 100 percent.

1. Your child(ren) with special needs _____%

2. Your other children _____%

3. Spouse or significant other _____%

4. Job/work/volunteering _____%

5. Friends and extended family _____%

6. Self _____%

7. Other _____%

Next, create a pie chart using the circle below by turning your percentages into appropriately sized sections of the pie. (For example, an activity that takes 50 percent of your energy would be half of the pie.) Label each section.

Figure 2.1: Current energy pie

Exercise 2.4: How I would like to spend my energy

Think about your energy pie again. What would those percentages look like in your *ideal* world? Go back through the list and assign new percentages to each category based on your ideal life. Refine or add categories as needed. Use the circle below to chart these energy allocations. Make sure they add up to 100 percent.

1. Your child(ren) with special needs _____%

2. Your other children _____%

3. Spouse or significant other _____%

4. Job/work/volunteering _____%

5. Friends and extended family _____%

6. Self _____%

7. Other _____%

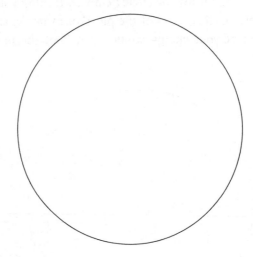

Figure 2.2: Ideal energy pie

Comparing our energy pies

The next step is to compare the current pie with the ideal pie and to observe what, if anything, is different. Many people are surprised to see their energy allocations in the first chart. While it usually isn't a surprise to see how little time they have for themselves, they are often surprised to find out how little energy their spouse is getting or how much of their energy is consumed by a variety of "shoulds", from keeping an immaculate house to volunteering for the latest school fundraiser.

Others find pleasant surprises. One mother's comment was typical of many responses we heard when she was relieved to see that her allocations of energy spent on her typically developing child didn't change much from the first chart to the second. She noted:

> I've been feeling so guilty about not spending enough energy on my other son but doing this chart made me realize that the amount of time and energy he gets is as much about him as it is about me. He is

15 – he doesn't want me butting into his life that much! The chart helped me see that I am spending a decent amount of time with him – probably more than he actually wants. It's a relief to be able to stop beating myself up about that.

Another mother found that even though her life was full of commitments such as volunteering in her child's classroom and teaching Sunday school, she actually enjoyed these activities and didn't want to cut back on them. This is a great example of how one person's burden is another person's pleasure.

Sometimes parents find that it is not amount of energy that is being allocated to a category that is the sticking point. It is the *quality* of the energy, specifically the frenetic and anxious thoughts that accompany the energy. Many parents comment that they don't want to spend less time with their children but they do want to enjoy their time with them more.

One mother noted:

I feel sad that I'm spending my time with Kelly the way I am. I'm more of her case manager than her mother. My time with her is more about therapy and work than laughter and play. I want to change my interactions and perceptions about time, not the actual amount of time with her.

As we move into the next part of the exercise, you can reflect on the story that your two pies are telling you.

Exercise 2.5: Comparing your energy pies

1. What did you learn from comparing your current and ideal energy pies? What were your biggest insights? Did anything surprise you?

2. Which areas of your life emerged as the ones that you most would like to change?

- Where do you want to spend less energy? What *specifically* do you want to do less of in this area? (E.g., I want to spend less time on my "other" category, which is largely housework and errands.)

- Where do you want to devote more energy? What *specifically* do you want to do more of in this area? (E.g. I want more time for myself. Specifically, I want time to write and play the piano. I would like to be able to spend an hour a day on those two activities.)

Exercise 2.6: Brainstorming possible solutions

Now comes the fun part – and the challenging part. We want you to get creative in thinking about how you can begin to make some of the shifts you have identified in your pies.

Here are some tips to get going:

- State what you want or don't want to do with your energy as clearly and in as much detail as possible. For example, rather than say, "I want to do something creative," you might say "I want to work on my jewelry designs at least one evening a week." Or rather than "I want to stop spending so much time in the car driving the kids everywhere," you might say, "I want to cut down my round trips in the car to no more than three per day." Being specific helps us get organized to meet our goals.

- When you are brainstorming ideas, don't edit yourself. Something that might feel unrealistic right now may be a great idea that just needs to be tweaked.

- Go for quantity. Brainstorm everything you can think of. You can whittle down the list later.

- Brainstorm as many little changes as you can. We have found that small incremental changes can make a huge difference in the perception of the quality of our life. They are also generally easier to implement and maintain than large changes. When we coach parents, we would much rather hear "I'm going to make time to call my best friend in California once a month" than "I'm going to spend two hours a day on myself" as a first goal. We know the first goal is do-able and will reinforce the principles of the energy pie. The second goal, while potentially do-able over time, would be hard for most people to achieve right away.

Questions:

1. Look back at the previous exercise and list your top three energy "drains".

2. Brainstorm at least five ideas to *lessen* the energy you spend on each of these three areas. Try to be as specific as you can be. For example, if your goal is to spend less time in the car driving the kids, some ideas might include: I can resign from the XYZ committee so I don't have to drive to the meeting every week; I can find people to carpool with to swim lessons; I can limit the kids' after-school activities to things they can ride their bikes to; I can look into having groceries delivered to the house rather than driving to the store twice a week.

3. Now look at the list of things where you would like to increase your time commitment. What specific things can you do to spend *more* time on the areas that are getting too little of your energy? Again, being specific is the key. Also, think about combining goals. For example: I want to spend more time with my friends and to exercise more, so maybe I can go on a hike with a friend once a month.

Exercise 2.7: Developing your plan

Go back to the previous exercise and look at the ideas you have brainstormed.

1. Of the things that I have listed, what could I do immediately?

2. Of the things that I have listed, what three actions can I take in the next week?

3. Are there any minor obstacles that I need to take care of before I can take the positive actions I've identified? (For example, if you want to begin running but you don't have running shoes that fit well, this will be an impediment until you take care of it.)

4. Who can I enlist to help me make sure that I follow through on these ideas? How can I use people in my circles of support to help me make some of these changes? (For example, you could have a brainstorming session with a friend, give her a copy of the list that you agree on and have her check in once a week.)

For some parents, these exercises bring up some unexpected emotions. Many parents shared some variation of the following:

I felt anxious doing the second chart. My life may not be perfect now but at least I know what I'm doing and it's all kind of working. If I start making changes, I'm afraid all those balls that I am juggling will drop.

This mother articulated a common underlying belief that often undermines our best attempts to make changes in our lives: "If I don't do what I have been doing, everything will fall apart." If you really believe that statement, how motivated can you be to make changes in your life?

In Chapter 4, we will examine those statements and learn how to reframe them into a more useful perspective. For now, we'd like to acknowledge that our beliefs about what we can or cannot do with our lives are important and can serve to unintentionally sabotage our best efforts to make changes.

Becoming aware of our "soft addictions"

Linda:

When I look at my pie chart, if I'm honest, I devote more energy than I feel good about to a category I call "numb-out time." For me, this often means watching TV at night after the kids are in bed, to have some peace and quiet. I picked up this habit when Miah was little and I felt I needed an escape from my worries about her.

I don't think there is anything inherently wrong with TV – just its overuse. I see that I can turn it on mindlessly as an easy escape from my real life. I got my own insight about my use of TV from author Judith Wright who, in her book *There Must Be More Than This* (2003), discusses how we sometimes use our routines to help us block our feelings. By doing so, we might feel like we are resting in the moment, but we may be zoning out of our lives and aimlessly filling our time. I know I sometimes use my "soft addiction" to keep me from feeling my true feelings or tapping into my deeper emotions.

I have found it immensely helpful to ask myself, "What do I need to help me better care for myself right now?" When I ask this question, sometimes I still turn on the TV. But sometimes I turn off the TV, pour a cup of tea and read a journal, take a bath, or talk with my husband. I find I am *more* content. TV, for me, might feel comforting sometimes and this is OK. But I want to be nurtured, and this "soft addiction" definitely doesn't do that! In fact, I know its mindless use leads me to a certain entropy, while other pursuits lead to moments of contentment and even joy. I want a life of fullness and awakening of my spirit, a life that is uplifting and deeply meaningful. So my resolve is to be *awake* about my choices.

If we can name our "soft addictions", decrease or eliminate them, we can build a more joyful life. The trick is to distinguish between soft addictions and activities that genuinely relax us, between escapist entertainment and possibilities for self-discovery. Most of us feel we sometimes need to get away and zone out for a while to avoid the stress of daily living. The problem with this is that the stress is still there when we come back to our lives. And these habitual activities aren't building us up to be better able to deal with our real life situations. Outlets are crucial, but we need to ask ourselves if our outlets have become habits that are squandering our precious time and energy in ways that aren't life-affirming.

Exercise 2.8: Looking at our own soft addictions

1. Notice what you do in your day. Look for things not identified on your earlier pie and in your energy drain list. Take a look at the list in Question 3 and see if any of these belong on your own list of "soft addictions" or energy drains. (Remember that none of these activities are "bad". Only you can decide if you are over-using them.)

2. Watch your behavior for the next several days and jot down what you notice about how your time is spent. Are you satisfied with how you are spending your time? What would you like to see change?

3. List what, when, and how you are going to eliminate or change your obstacles (e.g., limit television to no more than one hour per night or limit television to three nights per week, only check email three times per day – never on weekends). Remember that little steps work best! Here are a few ideas of what you might want to consider.

    •   Media: watching television, surfing the Internet, checking weather, news, reading magazines or newspapers, checking eBay

- Communications: phone calls, email, Instant Messenger, gossiping with friends

- Buying/Shopping: bargain hunting, hanging out in the mall, cruising garage sales

- Overdoing: over-eating, over-exercising, cleaning, caregiving

- Sleeping or napping too much

- Overworking, over-scheduling, over-committing in volunteer or other activities.

Most of these soft addictions are masks to stop us really experiencing our innermost feelings. They are resistance – a decision to say *no* to our current reality. Unfortunately, if left unchecked, resistance can last a lifetime.

Linda:
One mother that I worked with shared that she expressed her resistance by disengaging while doing anything related to her son's disability. She ate junk food while engaging in his therapeutic activities. She zoned out during meetings with professionals and boycotted any books or workshops on her son's condition. It was as if she was trying to ward off her feelings of pain about her son's condition by refusing to engage deeply. Unfortunately, the more she resisted, the more stuck and unhappy she became. Whatever we refuse to feel never goes away. In fact, it usually festers.

By realizing that she was using soft addictions to fuel her resistance, she was able to feel her pain, and over time, found it transformed and lightened. By actually experiencing her painful feelings instead of stuffing them or disengaging, this woman let her feelings surface.

Real shifts can only occur when we're honest with ourselves. Our soft addictions block us from our true feelings and, therefore, keep us from ourselves. Self-care is not about busying and distracting ourselves from our pain. As this mother so eloquently stated, "no more pushing it away... I feel sad about Chris and me, but by acknowledging it I feel hopeful somehow too...also a lot more real."

This mom found that her soft addictions were actually causing her resistance and pain to persist, not diminish. When she lived with her pain, she found that joy sprang forth not in spite of her sorrow, but paradoxically right along with it. Then she could tackle looking at her life honestly and building in real self-care strategies that energized her rather than just numbed her.

Exercise 2.9: Building more joy into our "must do" list

Sometimes our resistance may be that we have forgotten how to take care of ourselves, maybe even forgotten how to play. Albert Einstein, a man of great intelligence and insight, said that wholeness comes from seeking and seeing beauty in our lives, playfulness, and thoughtfulness. Maybe we have forgotten the sacredness of play. Sometimes building a joyful life simply means playing more. A spirit of play and spontaneity can fill our homes with fun.

This exercise looks at how we can infuse those mundane parts of our lives with more joy.

1. Make a list all the everyday things you must do during the course of a typical day.

2. How can play and love of life, self, and others be honored in these moments? (E.g., reading to your child a book you both enjoy while tube feeding, listening to your favorite music while cleaning the house, planting flowers with your child to work on sensory integration issues.)

Final thoughts

You count. You deserve a great life. Spending time on yourself is not selfish. In fact, one of the greatest gifts you can give your child is a happier and less stressed parent.

How does reading these statements make you feel? Hopefully, you feel inspired and galvanized to make your life exactly what you want it to be.

Still having a few doubts? Don't be concerned if you are not 100 percent sold just yet – the coming chapters will help you look at the underlying beliefs and attitudes that may be getting in your way.

For now, focus on the positive changes you have identified and try to move forward in a few concrete areas. Six months from now, challenge yourself to re-read this chapter. We think you will be thrilled with how far you have come.

> *No punishment anyone might inflict on us could*
> *possibly be worse than the punishment we inflict on*
> *ourselves by conspiring in our own diminishment.*
>
> *Parker J. Palmer (1999, p. 34)*

CHAPTER 3

The Twisted Skein:
Embracing Our Complex
and Conflicting Feelings

*We do not live an equal life, but one of contrasts
and patchwork; now a little joy, then a sorrow,
now a sin, then a generous or brave action.*

Ralph Waldo Emerson, poet and essayist, 1803–1882

Nancy:

Sometimes serendipitous things happen when you are writing a book. This chapter is a good example. Linda and I had great difficulty in coming up with a title that we felt captured the essence of the chapter – that special ability some people have of being able to fully experience their feelings, letting them wash over them in a conscious way but without fear of drowning. We knew what we wanted to talk about but couldn't seem to come up with a succinct way to describe it.

A few weeks after our discussion about the chapter title, we led a parent workshop. While we discussed the "Stages of Adjustment" chart that you will find later in this chapter, one mother of a young adult woman with severe developmental disabilities commented that her emotions usually didn't follow the linear and discrete stages of the chart suggests. Instead, she noted, she often feels all of the emotions outlined on the chart simultaneously. She said, "I think of my feelings about my daughter like a skein of yarn with many colors, all twisted together. I feel them *all* at the same time – sadness, anger, joy, acceptance. I don't have to choose one feeling."

We had our chapter title and metaphor. Our feelings about our children and their special needs are indeed complex. It is normal and, we believe, even healthy to be able to feel many things at once. Our love, our anger, our sorrow, and our joy are all mixed in together.

I also realized that part of my own challenge in writing the chapter was that I didn't consider this particular skill of feeling and accepting my emotions to be a particular strength of mine. For better or for worse, I'm pretty good at compartmentalizing my feelings and filing them away for a less busy day that never seems to come.

Around this time, I attended my niece's graduation from prep school. I sat with my brother and sister-in-law during the ceremony, half listening as the headmaster recognized the most outstanding seniors of the year with various awards. Finally, he reached the last award, the Headmaster's Trophy. As he began to describe the qualities of the student who was the winner, I saw my brother and sister-in-law exchange glances. At some point in his recitation, it became clear that the headmaster could only be describing Sarah and I watched with excitement and joy as my niece crossed the stage to accept the award. I was filled with happiness for her and her parents as people turned to congratulate them.

Once the moment passed, though, I became aware of a growing feeling in the pit of my stomach. The closest I can come to describing it is that it felt like homesickness, a kind of hollow, almost painful sensation. As the commencement speaker droned on, I had time to reflect on what I was feeling. Painful thoughts flooded in. "We're never going to have a moment like this with Kirsten. Who will celebrate with us? Who will congratulate us? We're just as good parents as they are but no one will ever see that. Kirsten will never know the glow of public recognition... ." I then began to look around at the well-heeled crowd attending the graduation ceremony and began feeling annoyed and angry at them as well.

I immediately began to push my negative thoughts away by replacing them with logical and "positive" replacements – that it was Sarah's day, that I knew nothing about the other people at the graduation and their lives, that Kirsten would go on to achieve her own successes in the world and we would celebrate – and guess what. None of it made any difference. I felt horrible. Then, I remembered this chapter and realized that I was having a twisted skein moment and that it was OK. It was OK to think uncharitable, self-pitying, even inaccurate thoughts. I didn't need to be scared of them or feel guilty about them. They just *were*, triggered by a happy event that happened to push my buttons about achievement, success, and recognition.

I'd like to tell you that the moment I realized this, my painful feelings dissolved, but in fact, they lasted most of the day and into the evening. I decided to just observe them and see what happened. About two hours into Sarah's graduation party that evening, I realized that I'd reached my limit for making small talk with strangers and went into a bedroom and laid down – not usually something I give myself permission to do during a party. The next morning I awoke feeling almost back to normal.

This experience was a revelation to me. I've spent a lot of years believing that certain feelings are OK and others are not. My loving, patient feelings, for example, were what a "good" mother was supposed to feel. My feelings of anger, despair, and self-pity were bad: an indictment of what a bad mother and an immature spiritual soul I was. Now I can see more clearly that all my feelings just *are*. They come, I experience them, and they change as the situation and my own inner barometer changes. I give them too much power when I pin them down, label them and pronounce them good or bad. Realizing this makes me simultaneously take my feelings more and less seriously. I give them credence but I also know that no single feeling defines who I am or my spiritual worth. I know that I will continue to feel many things as this journey continues. I will have a few shining moments along with some dark shameful moments. It's all part of the process and the reality of being human.

Linda:

When Miah was about eight months old, Mark and I went to the National Seashore in Texas for a vacation with family. While visiting the park, we watched a class of high school students eating lunch on the beach while enjoying their fieldtrip. I spotted a young man with Down syndrome eating with the teachers while the rest of the class sat several feet away enjoying each others' company. I was heartbroken and filled with fear as my mind rushed to visions of Miah at that age, eating with the adults while everyone else had what I thought of as a "normal" high school experience.

When we returned home, with tears in my eyes, I told this story to one of Miah's therapists to whom I had become quite close. She responded by saying that surely by the time Miah was that age things would be better and she would be with the crowd, etc... etc...

Despite her good intentions, I did *not* feel comforted. What I desperately needed was someone to hear my fear and pain and validate it. I carried a little hurt and resentment about her response for some time.

But looking back on this situation today, I see that what I needed even more than her validation was to accept my *own* experience of suffering. It was perfectly logical that observing that scene would make me feel horrible and would trigger feelings of tremendous fear and loss.

It took me several years feel okay about my wide range of feelings, especially the turbulent ones. And what I now realize is that when we can accept our own feelings, we naturally become more accepting of other people's points of view. When I'm feeling really centered, I can see that other people's feelings, like my own, are subject to change and are not set in stone. When I can relax and just *be* with my feelings, I'm much more likely to be sympathetic and take things less seriously and personally. I may feel upset or depressed or angry for awhile, but I know things shift when I'm aware.

So Miah's therapist, while doing the best she could in the moment, was probably upset by this scenario too, and by reassuring me, she was trying to assuage some of her uncomfortable feelings, perhaps to avoid feeling her own sadness for me and Miah.

I'm not always great at this kind of self-reflection and acceptance though. But I've discovered a little trick that I now use to tip me off to stop and notice what is going on inside me – an inner persona I've nicknamed "Tired Tory". Sometimes I lose patience with my kids, don't really want to be around them or anyone else actually, and even *yell* at times (my heavens!). I'm not talking about the legitimate "Juliana, I can't believe you just wrote on the new tiled wall with permanent marker!" kind of yell. I'm talking about losing my temper over something truly minor. This morning, for example, I yelled at Miah when she couldn't find her shoes. Since we *all* lose things a lot in my house, I needed to ask myself why I reacted this way. What is really going on? Sure enough, there was Tired Tory telling me she needs my attention.

I'm not going to beat myself up about this, but I am going to apologize to Miah when she gets home, and I am going to pour myself a cup of tea and reflect on my interior life, gently – *with love*. My soul is hungry for some nourishment and Tired Tory needs to be heard.

How we feel about our child's differences is a complex thing, influenced by many factors including our beliefs and attitudes about disability and illness, our spiritual beliefs, and our expectations about parenting.

Our feelings are also highly variable. Our feelings change over time but also from moment to moment. Sorting out those feelings and being able to "settle" into something reasonably consistent can be a huge challenge, especially for parents whose children's conditions are frequently in flux.

In our interviews and work with parents, we have noticed that the most resilient parents seem to be those who understand and accept the flux – those who can roll with the punches and accept their bad days along with their good days; their finest moments along with their toughest ones.

In fact, those who study resilience find that the ability to experience and reconcile conflicting and variable emotions, far from being evidence of dysfunction, is a hallmark of those with "survivor personalities". Al Siebert, author of *The Survivor Personality* (1996), provided the following insights about why experiencing a twisted skein of feelings is actually a positive indicator:

> When I ask survivors if there is any quality or trait that contributes most to being a survivor, they usually answer without hesitation. They say either "flexibility" or "adaptability". That makes sense, but then I wondered, "How do you *do* flexibility? What makes mental and emotional flexibility possible?"
>
> We find an answer in the writings of T.C. Schneirla, a scientist famous for his studies of animal behavior. After years of research, he concluded that for any creature to survive, it must have the ability to move toward or away from anything near it. ... Schneirla described the ability to approach as well as to withdraw as being a "biphasic pattern of adjustment"... Biphasic personality traits increase survivability by allowing a person to be one way or its opposite in any situation. To have biphasic traits is to be more adaptable rather than being "either one way or another". ... Pairs of biphasic, paradoxical, or counter-balanced traits are essential to a survivor style because they give you choice about how to respond... To respond in the

same fixed way to all situations reduces your ability to adapt to
changing events and circumstances. (pp. 28–9)

We also see that parents who are least accepting of their range of feelings
often seem to struggle more with their overall adjustment. For example, in
workshops, we frequently hear parents of less severely disabled children
expressing guilt at their own feelings of upset about their own situations
after they have listened to some of the stories of other parents. Their language is often revealing as they express this guilt – "I guess I have nothing to
complain about; my situation seems like nothing compared to what some of
you are going through."

While we understand that genuine "aha" of awareness and gratitude that
comes when we are able to put our own situation in perspective, too often
we hear an element of self-abasement in these remarks – "If my situation
isn't the worst, then I have no right to feel the way I feel about it. What a
weakling I am to feel so badly."

It is often the parents of the more severely challenged children who
reassure these parents that their feelings of grief and disappointment are just
as valid as anyone else's experience. They assure these parents that pain is
pain and that no one can or should judge another person's pain. We can
almost see the relief on the faces of the "guilty" parents to have their feelings
validated by a wise and compassionate fellow traveler on this difficult road.

It is part of our culture to want to rid ourselves of painful feelings as
quickly as possible. No one *likes* to feel bad and we Westerners seem to have
a particularly low tolerance for sitting with our painful feelings. For many of
us, the very idea of focusing on our pain seems unnatural and unhealthy, as
though we are wallowing in our misery instead of taking action.

There are times when paying excessive attention to our difficult feelings
becomes its own challenge. But, in our observations, most of us err on the
side of spending too little time exploring what our feelings may be telling us
and too much time wishing them away without examination.

Nancy:
I recently led a workshop which included many adoptive parents
whose children were seriously impacted by harmful behavior
during the birth mother's pregnancy and inadequate prenatal care.

As the group began to work individually on the reframing exercise in Chapter 4, I noticed one mother who looked particularly

distressed. I approached her and asked her if I could help walk through the exercise with her. She confided that she was stuck on the very first question of the exercise in which we ask people to share their painful thoughts about their child's situation. Her son, in addition to having Fetal Alcohol Syndrome (FAS), had also been diagnosed with bipolar disorder and ADHD. It was clear from her earlier remarks in the workshop that their home life was very challenging. She said with tears in her eyes, "If I say that his behavior makes me angry or that I feel like our lives have been ruined, it would be like I'm blaming him and it's not his fault. He didn't choose to have this condition."

My heart broke for this mom who not only had her hands full with a much loved but extremely difficult child but who could not even give herself permission to acknowledge her grief about the situation. I reassured her as best I could that having painful feelings about the situation did not in any way diminish her love for her daughter. We talked about the fact that we can love our kids more than anything in the world and still have times when we feel tremendous anger, frustration, and even rage towards them. In fact, *all* parents experience similar feelings at times. We never even got past Question 1 of the exercise, but I considered her to have made a major breakthrough when she was able to articulate her negative feelings about her daughter without feeling that it was a betrayal of her love.

Often we pick up our coping strategies for dealing with painful emotions from our families in childhood. These deep-seated patterns of responding can be hard to break without conscious effort. The next exercise is designed to help you look at your willingness or resistance to experiencing difficult emotions and some ideas for identifying and acknowledging your own "Tired Tory".

Exercise 3.1: Gently looking at our emotions

(You may want to write, color, or draw your answers.)

1. What feelings tend to be the most difficult for you to experience? What do you do to avoid experiencing those feelings?

2. How did your parents handle their difficult feelings? How did they encourage you to handle your difficult feelings? What messages did you receive about having strong and/or negative feelings?

3. Where do different feelings *live* in your body? In what part of your body do you feel joy? Sorrow? Fear? Shame? Excitement? Wonder?

4. What is your body saying to you right now? What feelings are you currently experiencing?

5. What clues does your body give you when you need to slow down and listen to your interior life?

Caring for our souls

Thomas Moore, a Jungian therapist and author of *Care of the Soul* (1992), suggests that paying attention to our unacceptable feelings – in fact, by treating them as if they matter deeply, can be an important aspect of caring for our souls and ultimately bringing wholeness to our lives. He offers the following metaphor about the importance of caring for our pain rather than rushing to suppress it or make it "better":

> The Greeks told the story of the Minotaur, the bull-headed flesh-eating man who lived in the center of the labyrinth. He was a threatening beast, and yet his name was Asterion – Star. I often think of this paradox as I sit with someone with tears in her eyes, searching for some way to deal with a death, a divorce, or a depression. It is a beast, this thing that stirs in the core of her being, but it is also the star of her innermost nature. We have to care for this suffering with extreme reverence so that, in our fear and anger at the beast, we do not overlook the star. (p. 19)

If we are willing to pay attention to suffering and not prejudge it, we may find that there is meaning and beauty in it. This is what Moore terms "caring for the soul."

Part of caring for our souls as parents of children with differences is to acknowledge that the dreams we had for our children before we knew of their challenges have not unfolded as we once thought they would. We believe that every parent experiences this grief to an extent; even so-called "typical" children will ultimately exhibit some characteristic or will make decisions that are at odds with the parents' conscious or unconscious fantasy of them. However, parents of children with special needs have a particularly large gap between their early assumptions and the reality of their children's lives, making these feelings more intense and painful.

This next exercise provides an opportunity for us to look at those dreams and expectations and how they have changed in the course of parenting our children.

Exercise 3.2: Acknowledging lost dreams

1. What were your assumptions about your child's life before you knew about his or her condition? Describe what you thought a happy, successful life would look like for your child at that point in time.

2. How has your child's illness or disability impacted upon those dreams? What is no longer possible?

3. How have your feelings about success and happiness changed as a result of your child's illness?

4. What, if any, positives have come out of your child's disability or illness?

Defending our negative thoughts

Moore writes that one "trick" in caring for the soul is to look with an open mind at the very thing we reject about our feelings and to then to take the side of the rejected element. We like to imagine that we have been handed the job of becoming our own passionate defense attorney for these maligned and despised feelings.

Most of us have some private feelings that we have deemed wrong, stupid, or childish in regard to our kids and their disability of illness. Some people criticize themselves for feeling badly when others seem to be dealing with more difficult situations with more grace. Others find themselves unable to stop worrying about the future. Some are horrified at the negative feelings they have towards their child. How can these feelings be understood in the context of our wholeness and how can accepting these feelings serve us on our road to building a joyful life?

Nancy:
One of my favorite movies is *Defending Your Life*. In this comedy, Albert Brooks plays Daniel Miller, a 40-something advertising executive who dies in a car crash while changing the CD in his new BMW on an LA freeway. When he awakens, he finds himself in a Southern California-like limbo where the "Big Brains" (the surprisingly bureaucratic personnel who run the place) will determine whether he has evolved enough to move onto the next spiritual plane or whether he needs to go back to Earth to do some additional work. This decision is made by a judge in a movie-theatre-like court room where the seminal moments of Miller's life are projected on the screen while the appointed prosecutor and defense attorney both attempt to prove his spiritual readiness (or

lack thereof) for the next evolution. While Brooks oozes mortification as a montage of his character's most humiliating moments plays on screen, Meryl Streep, his love interest, is in another courtroom for her own viewing, curled up in a big comfy chair and smugly reliving the many heroic moments of her life while her prosecutor and defense attorney praise and admire her.

In addition to being a truly funny movie, it was also thought provoking. What would be the key moments that I would use to evaluate to my own spiritual evolution? How would I defend my own life?

I saw this movie many years before Kirsten was born and at the time, I really had no sense of what my defining moments would be. Now, when I look back over the past five years of dealing with Kirsten's illness, I can identify particular moments that would provide both my defense attorney *and* the prosecutor with some serious fodder for arguing both sides of the case for my spiritual growth.

There is no doubt in my mind that some of the finest moments of my life have come in mothering Kirsten. There have been times when I have thought "Yes, that was the person I want to be – loving, kind, compassionate, even wise. I'm proud of who I am and how I handled that situation." Then there are the moments that make me cringe with embarrassment and regret. Moments when my own anger and resentment boiled over and culminated in harsh and hurtful words. When I assure Kirsten that even when people get angry with each other, they still love each other, I'm thinking of these moments as much as her outbursts. I forgive *her* trespasses easily. It's been harder to forgive my own.

One of my most "unacceptable" feelings is that I can have such intensely negative reactions to Kirsten's behaviors despite the fact that I understand that she is not always in control of her behavior. Yet, I find that I can't consistently rise above my own feelings of anger and hurt. This inability to react with compassion and love to her at all times makes me feel like a bad mother and an immature person.

In keeping with Moore's questions, I asked myself, "How can I defend my negative feelings?". To my surprise, several things came up rather easily. For starters, I realized that it's a sign of my own mental health that I find Kirsten's behavior upsetting and at times, enraging. I respect myself and expect to be treated decently by others, especially my loved ones. When that doesn't happen, I don't take it lightly.

I also saw that my anger gives Kirsten realistic feedback on how other people will respond to her undesirable behavior. If I never got angry with her, would she understand the consequences of such behavior outside the protected world of her family or would she expect that everyone should overlook her behavior on the basis of her illness?

It *would* be nice if my brain could overrule my emotions and I could rationalize away my feelings of anger by chalking her behavior up to her illness. And, in reality, I am able to do that much of the time. But, as I looked more closely, I saw that my expectation of *always* being able to do that – particularly when her behaviors have been going on for days, weeks or months – is asking an awful lot of myself. My reactions to her behavior show me that I am human and react like a person, not a saint. I don't have to label myself as immature simply because I'm not perfect.

Finally, my reaction to her behavior also helps me see how deeply connected I am to her. I am not a professional who can look at her clinically and analyze her behavior at arm's length. She is my child and she has the power to wound me with her words and actions. Her behavior also triggers my fears about her future and her capacity for intimate relationships. I can see that part of my anger is also fear because I love her so much.

So, the defense rests. But what was the verdict? I'm still not able to give myself a full pardon. But I found that after doing this exercise myself, I felt much less guilty about my negative reactions to Kirsten's behavior. It also let me focus my energy on other aspects of our negative interactions – such as how quickly I can recover my equilibrium and how well I can help her (and me) process what happened in a way that is truthful but positive. I help her more by modeling how people move past angry feelings, apologize and forgive than I can by trying to be a saint who never reacts to abusive or provocative behavior.

Exercise 3.3: Giving attention and space to our pain

1. What beliefs do you carry about how you should or should not feel about your child or their disability or illness? (For example,

"I should never be angry at Jenny's outbursts since she can't control them" or "I should be patient with how slow Sam is – it's not his fault that his body doesn't work right".)

2. Select a belief from your list that is particularly troublesome to you. Now imagine that a close friend comes to you feeling very guilty and confesses she has trouble with that very issue. What would you say to your friend to help her believe that she has a right to her feelings? Is there anything positive that you could imagine coming out of those feelings?

3. Now that you've had a chance to reflect on the positive aspects of one of your unacceptable feelings, do you feel differently? Is it easier to be compassionate with yourself and your perceived "shortcomings"? If you could stay in this place of acceptance, how might it change your feelings about your child or your child's situation?

Table 3.1: Common stages of adjustment

Stage	Common Feelings/Behaviors	Comments
Shock	Cry, feelings of dejection, may express feelings through physical outbursts or inappropriate laughter/comment	This is a normal reaction to a very difficult situation
Denial	Search for or try to propose various actions in attempt to change the reality; "shop for a cure" or bargain for a different reality	This stage is often an extension of stage one
Anger	May demonstrate anger outward, withdraw and become passive from feelings of guilt; may verbally attack or scapegoat others including diagnostician or other professionals	
Resignation	Overwhelming burden, shame, guilt, hopelessness, anxiety, depression	First sign of acceptance may be retreating; attempting to hide child from friends and others. Concern is with abnormal isolation
Acceptance	Unconditional positive regard for child; stronger skills in coping with life's trials as well as being able to help child, themselves, others; willing to become a team member	
More objectivity	Ability to imagine a positive future, talk of child without undue emotion	Regression to anger and frustration can occur, often due to insensitivity, lack of recognition and acceptance by others

Source: Adapted from Healey 1996, with permission

A framework for our feelings

At times, it can be difficult for parents to clearly articulate how we feel about our child. Our feelings are often in flux and, caught up in the midst of our internal chaos, it is hard to step back and look at what we are experiencing with any distance.

Frameworks can be a helpful way for us to make sense of our emotions and to see them in the broader perspective. The framework presented in Table 3.1 was developed by William C. Healy and adapts Elizabeth Kübler Ross's model of the stages of grieving after a death for parents of children who have differences.

While these stages are similar to Kübler Ross's model, there are some important differences. Most of our children's situations will not have the finality of a death. Grieving – or adjusting to – an ongoing situation requires different coping skills. What's more, the situation itself is usually not stable. Our children keep changing as they grow and develop and their growth and changes will in turn trigger many feelings in us as we live through each new development with them.

The limitation of this type of model is that it suggests that our feelings follow a neat linear path. But we all know intuitively that human emotion is rarely so orderly. This process of adjustment is different for each person. We may race through some phases and linger uncomfortably in others. We may think we have moved through one stage only to find ourselves back there again and again as various life events trigger deep feelings in us. And, as the mom at the beginning of the chapter so rightly noted, we may feel that we are in many stages simultaneously.

But the framework does allow us to put our feelings in a context; to see that there has been movement and progress in some cases and to reassure us that the stages ahead may allow us more joy and comfort.

Shock, the first stage, is often the predominant emotion we experience upon learning about our child's disability. Shock can take many forms. It can be that devastating moment after birth where everyone in the delivery room gets very quiet and the medical professionals whisk the baby away for tests and intervention. It can be a meeting with a specialist when a parent's worst fears about their child's health are confirmed. Or it can be a series of "mini-shocks" as the child's situation is slowly revealed through time, observation, and testing. One mom whose daughter has Down syndrome shared the following story of her shock and anger in the early days of her daughter's life:

It really was a shock when our daughter was born. The hardest thing that first day was making phone calls to our family and telling them that Claire was born with Down syndrome. We spent the whole next year in a fog trying to figure things out. Now that I look back, I think that one of the things that made me so angry in the beginning was just that I had done everything I could to have a healthy baby – she *was* healthy per se, she didn't have any heart defects or anything – but she was not born typically. And I just really was mad about that because I know and have seen other people who smoke through their pregnancies and did everything wrong and they have perfect babies. That was one of the things I really struggled with and then I came to the realization that really nothing is in our control. That is a pretty hard pill to swallow because I'm usually a person who pretty much takes things by the horns – here's a problem, we can fix it, – and that just really bothered me.

One mom whose son had been given the diagnosis of "global developmental delays" told this story of her own mini-shock:

I struggled with not feeling like we had a "real" diagnosis that explained what was going on with Chase but I guess I got used to hearing the term "global developmental delay". Then one day, I had to take him to the doctor for an ear infection or something and our regular doctor was out. The doc who was covering for our doctor called us in and in talking about Chase, referred to him as "mentally retarded". I just went into shock. I hadn't heard that term used to describe him before and I was devastated.

In talking with parents about their experiences during the shock phase, we were struck by how closely their experience mirrored people in physical shock. They report "being in a daze" or numb, unable to process information or make decisions. Unfortunately, professionals often miss the signs of shock and proceed to inundate parents with information and advice.

Denial, like shock, can take many different forms. When we hear the word "denial", the classic form of denial – a parent insisting that the diagnosis is wrong, that there is nothing wrong with their child, or that the issues have been blown way out of proportion – is usually what comes to mind. But denial can have other faces as well.

Nancy:

I stayed in denial for a long time. Only, I didn't know that it was denial. In fact, I thought I was dealing with Kirsten's problems pretty well – or at least very proactively. Once we accepted that her behavior showed no signs of magically disappearing as quickly as it had come, we jumped into action. Because of our concerns about medication, we had a long list of things we wanted to investigate before consulting a psychiatrist. We went from an occupational therapist to behavioral therapy to alternative nutrition to bodywork without any success.

Even after we were given a "real" diagnosis of bipolar disorder, my quest for the cure didn't let up. I read everything I could find about bipolar disorder, the various medications, and the current research. I believed that if I knew enough, I could somehow fix the situation. I equated my frenetic activity with hope and caring. If I tried hard enough, all would be well.

Now, I can look back and see that all my activity was a form of denial. I was saying the words "Kirsten has bipolar disorder" but my thinking went something like this – "if I try my hardest and learn everything there is to know, we will find something that will work and then our lives can return to normal again."

I actively sought to block out anything that threatened my ability to look at Kirsten's illness through my own "we can fix this" lens. This particular coping strategy backfired on me when I attended a local support group meeting for parents with bipolar children. I listened with horror to their stories of their children's struggles, went home, and literally took to my bed. I was so upset by this intrusion of reality into the positive story I had constructed for myself that I had to distance myself immediately from these families by reassuring myself that Kirsten's issues would never be so severe.

Eventually it became clear (even to me) that all my attempts to "fix" Kirsten were not going to cure her illness. I had to find a way to live my life with her illness. While I pretty much skipped through anger, I spent a lot of time in resignation – or in my case, depression. I couldn't accept how compromised my life was and how hopeless it all felt to me.

I was able to move out of my depression and into a more accepting and objective place. But it is stunning to me how easy it is to slip back into earlier stages. When Kirsten is doing well, I happily wallow in denial. When things are awful, I spend a few days in depression, sure that I will never have a happy moment again. But, with the distance of some years and some hard work, I now know to anticipate that these times won't last forever. I've learned to trust my own ability to cope.

It is very common to have partners experience these stages at very different speeds and intensities. This can be both difficult and helpful. It's a wonderful thing when partners are able to balance one another. The partner that is feeling more optimistic provides support and encouragement to the one that is feeling down. Or the parent who is ready to give up is refueled by the angry energy of the other partner who wants to take on the world.

Being out of sync on stages can also be extremely painful for partners. One spouse accuses the other of over-reacting to minor problems. The other spouse is infuriated at what she sees as the other partner's inability to look at the child's problems realistically. One partner wants to go along with the doctor's recommendations while the other is in a rage with the entire medical profession. These imbalances can lead to serious relationship problems if they are not addressed.

Linda:
My husband, Mark and I played this out in spades when Miah was a baby. The first few weeks after her birth, I cried and cried or sat despondent on the sofa, painstakingly trying to feed her. Mark, on the other hand, sprang into action, making appointments for Miah while still running his own business and our household. A few weeks later, he became depressed and sullen while I was full steam ahead with doctors' appointments and plans, but totally unaware of my own anger.

On our first "date" after Miah's birth, we decided to go for a hike. As we walked, Mark talked openly for the first time about how difficult our situation felt to him. In his fear and sadness, he worried aloud that he wasn't sure he was up for the task.

His vulnerable confession terrified me and threatened my fragile sense of safety and stability. I snapped, "Be a man!" at him, in essence, telling him that he was not allowed to have (or at least express) his feelings of sorrow and being overwhelmed.

What I didn't realize at the time was that he was only venting his grief in that moment. He loves our life and wouldn't trade Miah for the world. How I wish I could have seen that then and supported him more compassionately, knowing that stages change and our feelings evolve.

We've come a long way since then. What has helped us the most, I believe, is "checking in" with each other often. Most of us have emotional lives that are messy, filled with unexpressed feelings and unmet needs. Mark and I regularly ask each other where the other one is on a particular issue or in general. These conversations really help cut out the agony of thinking you know what someone else is feeling. I'm often surprised at how wrong I am.

Of course, checking in with oneself needs to come first... Obviously, I hadn't checked in with myself that day long ago when I lost my cool and compassion. By checking in we now navigate through feelings with each other and hopefully are more emotionally present and loving.

One thing that is common among all parents we have met is that the early years of their adjustment were filled with a huge range of emotions and these emotions often shifted radically from week to week and month to month.

When Robbie was first diagnosed he was 2½. Being the kind of person I am, I said, "Let's get going on everything possible". Within a month I had him signed up for occupational therapy, home program, and speech therapy. Immediately, my reaction was to *do* something. I would say that I was pretty much in the "don't talk to me and don't bother me, I'm working on my child" mode for at least for the first six months.

After that first six months I think it really started to sink in that this wasn't going to change overnight, and that I wasn't going to fix it in six months or a year. Rather, this was going to be a long term reality. I think for the next six months I was pretty depressed. I cried a lot. I slept a lot. I was very angry. That mostly came out to the people I felt safe with – my sister, my husband, my mom. It was my sister actually who pointed out how angry I was and talked to me about what really was going on. I think having her point out that I was angry and really talking to her about what I was angry about helped me see that some of my anger really wasn't anger – it was just fear. Not knowing what was going to happen. That really helped. But for the first year I was kind of a basket case.

Through that first year having a home program provider was amazing because she would often program me into Robbie's sessions. I think that is why I began to realize that this was a family affair. It isn't just me and it isn't just him. We all have to work together. I started really learning from her how to work with Robbie, how to be more directive with him, how to break the task down into really tiny pieces so that he could learn one simple thing at a time.

I would say that it probably took me a good year and a half to two years before I started to recognize that we had to figure out a way to integrate Robbie's condition into our life as a family. We can't stop going out to eat, we can't stop going on trips, and we can't stop living just because we have a kid with issues.

Exercise 3.4: Your stages of adjustment

1. Review the stages of adjustment (Table 3.1) again. Where do you think you are in your own adjustment to your child's situation?

2. What are your biggest concerns for yourself (not your child) as you move through these stages?

3. What situations or events tend to trigger feelings from earlier stages?

4. What could others do to help you as you move through these stages?

Moving towards acceptance and the challenge of transitions

Tom Sullivan, the author of *Special Parent, Special Child* (1996), has also researched the reactions of parents to their children's illnesses or disabilities. He notes that as parents pass through the early stages of grief and shock, most begin to accept their child's situation and adjust to it. He also notes, however, that this initial level of acceptance is often relatively fragile and can be fraught with its own challenges.

One of the common reactions he sees in parents who are moving towards acceptance is that they can begin to over-identify with their child's disability or illness so much that it can lead to the loss of their own identity. Sullivan receives hundreds of letters from parents who refer to themselves as "the parent of..." instead of by their names. He wrote that they see themselves as the parent of a child with a disability, rather than a whole human being. He added that he never seemed to learn anything else about the parent. Yes, they are accepting – even embracing – their child's situation, but at a huge cost to themselves.

We've also noted that in the later stages of adjustment that regression back to earlier stages of grief, anger or depression were often triggered by external circumstances rather than the objective reality of the child's situation. Many parents spoke about the pain that they felt seeing their child excluded socially. While the family and close friends may have adjusted to their child's differences, the reaction of the rest of the world can still have the power to wound and enrage.

One mom commented, "I once went into my daughter's school to drop something off around lunch time and peeked into the lunch room and saw her sitting alone. It just about killed me."

Another mom remembered with pain watching a musical performance at her daughter's school at the end of a social studies unit on Alaska:

> Amy was the only child in the class who did not have a special part in the performance. Because she didn't have a special part, they even forgot to put her name on the program. Even her 4-year-old sister asked "why isn't Amy getting to do anything?" I don't think my daughter really noticed what had happened but I went home and cried for 20 minutes.

Linda:
> When Miah was born, an elderly family member lamented that her birth was more difficult to deal with and accept than her own child's stillbirth had been. This was extremely hard for me to hear and hurt me to the core. Her words kept me up at night, "My baby's birth was more tragic to her than her own child's death!" She visited recently and said something similar. I mentioned loaning a book to a woman who is expecting a child with Down syndrome, and my relative again talked of not being able to cope with or ever want a child with a disability. I was again stunned and a little hurt. But I quickly remembered our conversation from years ago. I felt so much lighter now. I was able to feel her fear around disability and my overwhelming emotion was sadness *for her.* I feel disappointed she will probably never appreciate Miah, but very lucky that I can. Sadness swept over me, but sleep came easily that night.

Transitional times tend to be particularly vulnerable times for many parents. Transition to middle school, high school and independent living are cited by many as particularly stressful times. Changes in the level of support the child receives or changes in the social structure of the new situation often generate tremendous anxiety for parents.

Transitions frequently have "events" associated with them such as graduations and celebratory parties and these too can cause pain. Consciously or unconsciously, we all have our own mental images of life's big moments and what they will be like for our children: the first day of school, the school play, scoring the winning goal in the soccer finals, the senior prom, high school graduation, taking our kids to college. Inevitably, even when those days are filled with joy, they also trigger feelings of loss, fear, and sadness that our fantasy is not exactly matching our reality. These feelings, in turn, can send us reeling back to an earlier stage of adjustment.

For other parents, the transitions are less external. The child's illness or disability may progress to a new level that requires more extensive treatment or intervention. It may limit both the child and family in new ways. These transitions also must be acknowledged and grieved by the parents and this grieving process usually involves revisiting an earlier stage of adjustment.

The good news is that most parents who are farther along in their stages of adjustment find that they move through these earlier emotions much more quickly than we were able to the first time through. They still experience all the feelings but they last for a few days or weeks as opposed to months or years. These parents also benefit from the experience of having had sustained periods of resolution and acceptance in the past. This provides the perspective and confidence that their painful feelings will pass in time and that they are simply part of the whole process.

Integration

In talking with our resilient families, we found that their adjustment to their child's special needs never resulted in feeling like their lives were perfect and pain-free – whose lives are, after all? Nor did they deny that their children's disability or illness made life more challenging. What did change was their ability to integrate their child's situation into their lives in a way that felt natural and comfortable.

One mother whose son had speech and language delays explained:
Part of this progression is time passing. You have to adjust to big life changes like marriage. Having a child with special needs was kind of like a big life change because I had written the script of this kid and I realized that I really couldn't do that because we don't know what our future is. I let go of the script. I just let him go.

At first, I went so far into literature that I was saturated and I saturated my psyche. That wasn't a very happy time. I did that until I felt like I was an expert. Finally, I was able to let go of that. I realized that the literature wasn't my child and it didn't describe my child. I learned about the limitations of thinking in categories. We also made a choice not to have an IEP [Individual Education Plan] because we didn't think it would really help him. We have done it more free form.

My advice is to find parents with whom you feel very comfortable. Find people that don't make you feel different or apologetic. Strike that good balance for yourself. I think it is really easy to get depressed and feel stuck. It is your choice to take it back. We all deserve a good life and balance in our life. We all deserve support. Wherever you find you are comfortable and happy is important. I see parents in the state of trauma I was in. I offer them support and advice and encouragement and I also tell them that they will not feel this way forever. They will have moved. You will integrate and adjust and accept. Denial can have an impact that may delay the movement. You can also feel hopeless. I think if you live in the moment well, that helped me move through it faster. Grieving was an important thing for me to do to make it through. We are more open with others now. Acknowledging where we are at is helpful. I feel much better being open. I feel more accepting of him and myself.

Another mom whose daughter has cognitive disabilities described her own evolution as follows:

My emotional state now is 100 percent for accepting who she is. I totally accept her for the person that she is. I would say that there is a 5 percent part of me that fears for her future. Initially I would say I was 40 percent concerned with her future. My worry has decreased because I see the skills that she has gained. I see her making connections with people, showing a true interest in school, a true interest in reading, music, food. All of those good things in life. She has those basic joys. I see her being independent and I can see her living on her own.

I think it would be so easy to get wrapped up in your child with a disability. You just have to let that go. You can't hover over them all of the time. It is important for them to know that they have allies in the world. I am very open to having people enjoy my child. Why shut people off from being around my child? It is really important to be open. She is mine, but she is also part of the community and she wants to embrace the community and I need to allow the community to embrace her back.

We have found that many parents at the acceptance stage of their adjustment, while not a formal part of the stages of adjustment model, become advocates and even activists for change. Instead of shrinking from the world's judgment, they challenge it head on through related volunteer work, career changes, and political activism. They move from "there is something wrong with my child" to "there is something wrong with a community/country/world that doesn't accept and value my child." This can be a very empowering place for both the parent and the child who sees the parent advocating their rights and affirming their value to the world.

Cultivating a sense of lightness

There are times when nothing seems funny and it feels like we will never laugh again. While we would never suggest that we mask deep pain with humor, we do believe that cultivating a sense of lightness is integral to building a joyful life. We were interested to find research that proves that laughter is literally healing. Medical researchers at Loma Linda University in California found that laughter increased natural killer cell activity (NKA) and lowered epinephrine, and cortisol levels. (Natural killer cells or NKAs are responsible for the early recognition and removal of virus and tumor cells. Elevated levels of epinephrine and cortisol are known to be immunosuppressive.)

Al Siebert, the author of *The Survivor Personality* (1996), also equates the ability to laugh at a situation to having internalized its lesson at an emotional level. He writes:

> Laughing about something learned is an excellent sign that valuable learning has occurred. Learning that results in personal growth is emotional as well as mental. The kind of learning associated with increasing life-competence happens in the body, not just in the mind. (p. 20)

Nancy:
If I had to choose the single quality that has helped me the most in living a joyful life, it would have to be sense of humor. I simply can't imagine how John and I would have gotten through some of the more difficult times without having the ability to laugh.

I remember once reading the parable "Welcome to Holland" by Emily Perl Kingsley, who is the parent of a child with Down syndrome. Kingsley was making an analogy that giving birth to a child with Down syndrome was like planning a trip to Italy and then finding that you had landed in Holland. Her point was that although you are initially disappointed that you are in Holland instead of Italy, that when you take the time to look around you begin to see how beautiful Holland is and you begin to appreciate the trip you are taking instead of the one you thought you were taking. It seemed like a nice sentiment and I decided to read it aloud to John hoping it might provide some inspiration.

He listened patiently, if unenthusiastically. When I finished reading, we looked at each other and then I said "Holland! I *like* Holland. What I want to know is how we ended up in Afghanistan?" From that time on, geography became our own private little joke and shorthand metaphor for how things were going at a particular point in time. "Well" one of us will say, "the day started out in Baghdad but I think we're in Luxemburg now – a little bit boring but stable." It's a lot more fun than the usual 1 to 10 scale that we are asked to use on rating charts and it makes us laugh.

Linda:

Like Nancy, I would have to say humor is *key* to building a joyful life. Even in the worst of times, humor and laughter have helped heal my pain. One of my most joyful memories actually occurred a few days after my sister died. All my family was gathered at my brother's house and my family was supposed to divide up my sister's jewelry. My brother-in-law was a jeweler so she had a lot. We all laughed, told stories, and vied for particular pieces in a jovial way. It was like a piece of heaven, actually. I am so thankful we were not afraid to step back from our grief and laugh, anyway. It was truly a healing experience.

Little things make me laugh too… the bumper sticker that reads "Why two forks?" and most of my husband's jokes. And Miah makes me laugh. Thank goodness. I chuckle right now as I think of the time our family was in Denny's having breakfast when a young woman with a developmental disability herself sat behind us and began to make noises. Miah was scared to death! The irony was hilarious! Or the time her precocious and sometimes cocky younger sister ran through the house bawling, "I thought *I* was the smarter one!" after Miah answered a United States map question that had stumped her. The list goes on and on. I find that laughing with and at myself and my family increases my capacity for openness and feeling joy. In fact, I don't think I'm ever closer to people than when we are laughing together.

Exercise 3.5: Healing through laughter and play

1. What are some funny memories you have involving your child's situation?

2. What makes you laugh?

3. How can you cultivate more of this in your life?

4. What do you and your child do together that is fun? What else could you do?

Final thoughts

Giving yourself the space and permission to fully experience your feelings can be difficult when those feelings are painful. It may help to remember that in the midst of your toughest times, acknowledging and owning these emotions is an essential part of moving forward.

Carol Staudacher, in her book *A Time to Grieve* (1994), makes the following point:

> When we suffer any blow, we need to recover, to heal. Grief is the way to healing after a loss. When we are feeling deep, powerful emotions or impulses, it is necessary for us to acknowledge them, knowing they will not harm us. We won't damage ourselves or fall apart if we allow ourselves to feel and act in ways that are dictated by our truest instincts. We cannot constantly hold back, push away, or censor what we really feel. Fearing to grieve gets us nowhere. With grief, the way back is through. (p. 2)

If you are in the earlier stages of adjustment to your child's situation, feel free to ignore any and all helpful advice about staying positive, keeping a stiff upper lip, and being brave. Focus instead on really *feeling* what you feel and take comfort in the knowledge that there are brighter times ahead for you and your family.

> *Your joy is your sorrow unmasked.*
> *The deeper that sorrow carves into your being,*
> *the more joy you can contain.*
>
> *Kahlil Gibran (1978, p. 29)*

CHAPTER 4

Seeing with New Eyes: Reframing Our Perceptions and Beliefs

*The real voyage of discovery consists not in
seeking new landscapes, but in having new eyes.*

Marcel Proust, French novelist, 1881–1922

Nancy:

As a child I was fascinated by those black and white pictures that could be viewed in two entirely different ways. One picture in particular sticks in my mind – an ink blot that looked like a beautiful young woman when seen from one perspective and the face of an ugly old witch when seen from another. I recall that the first time I looked at the picture, I could only see the young woman. Someone had to literally show me how I could see it as a witch. "See, here is her nose, here is her chin, and there is her hood." And, strangely enough, once I was able to see the witch, I had trouble seeing the young woman again. It took me a while to be able to go back and forth between the two pictures, focusing at will on whichever version I wanted to see.

I've been thinking about the experience of seeing the same image two very different ways while writing this chapter. The ability to reframe necessitates the ability to see things from more than one perspective at the same time, yet this is not always an easy thing to do. Often when we begin working with reframing, we find that our initial perspective on a situation is the only one that we can see. It can be hard work to see it from another angle. Sometimes we need someone else to help us see our situation in a new light. Even then, the new perspective can feel artificial or uncomfortable.

Linda can attest to the fact that I was not a natural at reframing when we first began to develop our workshop exercises. It's not that I couldn't come up with alternative ways of looking at my situation – it was that I had trouble latching onto a new perspective that felt genuine and honest. At times, I was startled to see how tightly I clung to some of my negative perceptions. But, with her guidance, I learned that I could dig a bit deeper until I discovered what was really bothering me. And once I understood that, I could usually find a way of shifting my thinking in a more productive direction.

With practice, I've gotten to a point where I can mentally toggle back and forth between various ways of seeing without having to stop and walk myself through the process step by step. Occasionally, I have very satisfying moments when I notice that my brain begins to automatically sift through alternatives and select one that feels more positive and affirming than my initial thought. On the other hand, I still find situations where I don't particularly want to let go of my negative state of mind. Sometimes, for example, I don't feel like reframing my perception and it just feels good to write someone off as a jerk. And that's OK. The point of reframing for me is not to try to eradicate every negative feeling I experience but it does provide me with the skills to shift my frame of mind when I choose to do so.

Linda:

There is a famous story about a Chinese master painter painting a landscape. Just as he was about to finish, a drop of ink fell on his canvas. The young disciple who had been studying under him gasped, believing the scroll was ruined. But, without hesitating, the master took up his finest brush, and used the ink that had fallen to paint a delicate dragonfly hovering in the foreground of the landscape.

This story speaks to me profoundly as I make decisions about how I want to think and feel about my life. Like Nancy, I always felt I would have a good life and I never wanted to trade places with anyone. After my daughter was born, I struggled with sadness and anger. What, I wondered, would I do with this hand I've been dealt? I *wanted* to believe my life would still be great, but didn't always feel optimistic.

When Miah entered elementary school I found my worries increasing instead of decreasing. After several bad experiences at school around social interactions, I found myself worrying incessantly about how she was managing at school. I was depressed, tired, and depleted. I thought about the possibility that she was alone on the playground, about the child who refused to hold her hand at circle time, and about how the other kids were or weren't including her.

I decided to see a "life coach" who had the reputation for helping people get "unstuck" because I felt sick and tired of feeling sick and tired! I was doing all I could to help Miah establish friendships – hosting play-dates and talking with school personnel about facilitating friendships – but the worry was exhausting me.

During one appointment, the coach pointed out that my feelings were reasonable, but asked whether they were serving me or my daughter. It was then that I realized my thoughts weren't helping, but were instead exacerbating my feelings of sadness. I also saw that I might actually be hurting my daughter by conveying my worry to her. Miah sometimes shut down when I asked her, "How was your day? Who did you sit with at lunch?" I had thought her lack of response meant it was a bad day, but could it be that she was picking up on my lack of trust in her ability to make friends? Now I believe the best thing I can do for her is model how to be a good friend and then let her go for it! She does have all it takes to be liked. "You are likable just as you are! I trust you and your abilities!" are the messages I want to think to myself and convey to her. I still worry occasionally, but the incessant nature of my painful thoughts is gone.

I began to look at my thoughts and see them for what they were: thoughts and not necessarily truths. I worked on reframing them in ways that helped me articulate my greater truths and values about myself, my daughter, and the world. I began to see that, in fact, my daughter is quite happy. And guess what? I'm quite happy too.

One of the comments we often hear from parents is that their energy is not only depleted by the time they spend with their children but by the constant background worry. One mom commented, "I'm constantly thinking about my daughter even when I'm not with her. Is she happy? Does she have anyone to sit with at lunch? Did the nurse remember her med change? It's exhausting, even when I'm not with her."

No wonder the idea of freeing up energy for more fulfilling activities seems impossible to some parents. Even their "free" time is consumed with their concerns about their child.

As the energy pie exercise in Chapter 2 illustrates, there are a number of concrete things people can do to make changes in their lives. But even the most comprehensive list of ideas will prove difficult to put into action unless we also address the underlying thoughts and beliefs that drive our emotions. The objective of this chapter is to reframe the underlying messages we tell ourselves.

Sometimes it is healthy to accept our unhappy feelings and be gentle with ourselves until the darkness passes. But at other times, we find that these feelings are consuming us in unhealthy ways. David Burns, M.D., in *The Feeling Good Handbook* (1999), suggests we explore the following questions to help identify when we should accept our feelings and when we might want to work on reframing them:

- Have I been feeling this way for a long time?
- Am I doing something constructive about the problem, or am I simply brooding and avoiding it?
- Are my thoughts and feelings realistic?
- Am I making myself unhappy about a situation that's beyond my control?
- Are my expectations for the world realistic?
- Are my expectations for myself realistic?
- Am I feeling hopeless?
- Am I experiencing a loss of self-esteem? (p.63)

A "yes" answer to any of these questions suggests that reframing may be helpful. Even though we may be convinced our thoughts are 100 percent valid, some of our negative thoughts are likely to be distorted or unrealistic. Reframing helps us identify the attitudes we want to hold and gives us a way to change those automatic, unexamined thoughts that upset us. When we consciously reframe situations that upset us, we are better able to *act* or *accept*. It moves us beyond the stuck place and opens up new possibilities.

Fear/Love chart

When we are able to step back and look at emotions objectively, we can see them as information. They help us understand what is working and not working in our lives. They are intended to make us listen. Viewed in this light, they are not inherently bad or good. They just are.

Many psychologists believe that most of our emotions can be traced back to one of two core emotions – fear or love. And within these two emotions, we can be on the passive or active end of the spectrum. As the chart in the next exercise illustrates, when we are in a state of active love, our emotions and actions reflect this. We are able to educate, advocate, inspire, and lead. In a state of passive love, we are able to let go, forgive, accept, and embrace. In active fear, we seek to control others through criticism, manipulation, aggression, or nagging. In passive fear, we are mired in emotions such as victimization, resentment, being overwhelmed, worry, and anxiety.

Exercise 4.1: Looking at the roots of our emotions

Take a minute and look at the Fear/Love chart below.

	Love	
P a s s i v e	Allowing Softening/Accepting Loving self Letting go/Forgiving	Creating/Educating Advocating Developing + Solutions Loving others
	Being a victim Feeling sabotaged Feeling overwhelmed Worrying Resenting	Controlling others Manipulating others Criticizing Ridiculing Gossiping
	Fear	

Figure 4.1: Fear/Love chart

Write down any other emotions or behaviors into the relevant quadrants of the Fear/Love chart. We will come back to this chart as we begin to work with reframing our thoughts.

Reframing

The central tenet of the school of psychology known as cognitive therapy is that our emotions are caused by our thoughts. Consequently, if we change the thought behind the emotion, eventually the emotion will change as well. While this shift doesn't occur instantaneously, practitioners of this approach, known as cognitive behaviorists, believe that with time and practice, many painful emotions can be softened or even transformed by changing the underlying thoughts.

The ability to change underlying thoughts is also called *reframing*. Its first formal use was by family therapists who were trying to help people develop new thought patterns. Steven Wolin, M.D. and Sybill Wolin, Ph.D. (1999) are the directors of Project Resilience and have spent many years researching the role of reframing in people's ability to develop healthy coping strategies. They note:

> We all have stories about ourselves. The organizing themes of some people's stories are constructive. Other stories are destructive. The technique of reframing capitalizes on the subjective nature of personal stories to uncover underlying, underemphasized themes in people's stories that are potentially helpful. Its purpose is to arrive at an authentic and helpful story, one that does not eliminate the pain that hardship can cause but that also includes the strength that is forged in the struggle to prevail.

For example, a person who lived through an abusive childhood might have the following story:

> My parents were cold, unloving and abusive. I grew up feeling worthless and fearful. This has made it impossible for me to get close to other people.

However, another person with a similar background could frame his story this way:

> My parents were cold, unloving and abusive. But I survived my childhood even though it was very hard. Now I figure that if I could live through that experience, I can live through anything.

These are very different stories and you can imagine how differently the tellers feel about themselves. The goal of reframing is to help us retell our stories in a way that makes us feel empowered and resourceful. In our discussions with parents, we've found that the most resilient parents are those who, either through natural inclination or conscious effort, have been able to create the most positive stories about themselves and their children.

Because reframing is one of the most important tools we use throughout this book, we encourage you to spend as much time as you need on this chapter to feel comfortable with the technique.

Your initial thoughts

Reframing begins with an initial thought or statement. This is the thought that we would ultimately like to reframe – the thought that makes us feel bad, that keeps us up at night, or that leads us to worry constantly about our kids even when they are off doing something else.

> *Linda:*
> My painful thoughts tended to be about Miah's social life. Friends are extremely important to me and so when I was worrying about Miah, that's where my thoughts went. Here are some of the thoughts I would have about Miah:
>
> - Miah won't have any friends.
> - Kids are cruel.
> - Miah has trouble communicating.
> - What will her future be like? Happy? Lonely?
>
> These thoughts would consume me to the point where I would spend much of my day worrying about her and wondering how things were going. It was exhausting for me and it didn't help her at all. In fact, I think she picked up on my anxiety and it made her less confident in her own abilities to connect with other people.

Exercise 4.2: Identifying your painful thoughts

1. Without editing yourself, write down any difficult thoughts that come to mind about your child or something related to your child's disability or illness.

2. Look back at the Fear/Love chart in Exercise 4.1. Into which quadrant do most of these feelings fall?

Ultimately, we are going to work on reframing these thoughts. But first, we want to spend some time on the initial statements. We often find that when a parent is struggling to find a way to reframe a painful thought, it is because the initial statement about that thought is written in a way that makes it difficult to change. The initial statement can be like the first layer of the onion. Sometimes it needs to be peeled back before the statement can be reframed in a meaningful way.

We'd like to share an example from one of our workshops to illustrate this point. This mom, whose daughter has developmental delays that impact her speech, wrote the following statement:

Olivia can't communicate.

Olivia's mother found she was having great difficulty reframing this statement. "How can I reframe this genuinely? Saying that she *can* communicate doesn't make it true," she said. We asked her, "How does your statement make you feel? Where on the Fear /Love chart would you place those emotions?" We wanted her to clarify her initial statement by focusing on identifying the emotion behind the thought. She replied that it made her feel sad and also scared that something might happen to her daughter, but her daughter wouldn't be able to tell her what had happened.

Next we asked, "Is your statement literally true? Is Olivia unable to communicate?" The mom replied "No, not really. She does let me know when she's upset but she just can't tell me verbally." "How does that make you feel?" we asked. We continued this process until she felt that she had reached the truth of her feelings about her daughter's communication challenges. At that point, she reworked her initial statement as follows:

> I feel sad that Olivia can't communicate with me verbally because I am missing out on the fullness of communication I would like to have with her.

We will come back to her reframed statement in a moment. For now, notice that the way she revised this statement moved it from a definitive statement to one that was more specific and included her emotions. Once she restated her thought in this manner, she found it much easier to come up with reframing alternatives that felt true.

Exercise 4.3: Refining your initial statements

1. Of all the painful thoughts you identified in Exercise 4.2, select three statements that are the most upsetting to you. These are the thoughts you can work on reframing.

   (a)

   (b)

   (c)

2. The way that we write a statement can help or hinder our ability to reframe it. Definitive statements are often the most difficult to reframe. Select one of the three statements you have chosen and rewrite it using an "I" statement that contains the same issue but focuses on how *you* feel about the situation. For example, the initial statement "Jacob will never be able to live independently,"

might become "I am afraid that Jacob will never be able to live independently."

Sometimes when we focus on our feelings about the statement, we find a deeper layer that we want to express. For example, we might find that the statement "I am afraid that Jacob will never be able to live independently" might evolve to, "I am afraid that Jacob will never be able to live independently. I feel resentful that I may not get to enjoy a childfree retirement."

Reframing your painful thoughts

We're now at the point where we are going to work on reframing those painful thoughts by identifying alternative ways to view them or the situation they evoke. Because we've found that reframing can be tricky, here are some tips that may be helpful as you work on your statements.

- Take a look at where your statements fall on the Fear/Love chart in Exercise 4.1. Can you think of actions that you can take within the *active* love quadrant? Are you satisfied with your efforts in this area? Is there more you can do to educate, enlighten, advocate, or support? If your answer is "no", that's fine; many of us rightly feel we are already doing our best given our child's needs and our own resources.

- Can you reframe your statements to tap into the *passive* love quadrant by selecting statements that:
    - lessen some of your fear and worry?
    - inject love for yourself, your child, and others into your thoughts?
    - allow you to think from a position of compassion?

- Ask yourself, "What can I tell myself that makes me feel more hopeful? What will help me take action?" This is a chance to be gentle with yourself.

- Write your reframed statements in the present tense.

- Experiment with several alternatives. Sometimes it takes several tries to find a reframed statement that feels right. Often our reframed statements don't feel completely true right this minute. That's OK – they are meant to reflect our aspirations – what we would *like* to feel. But, it is important to choose something that feels honest and moves us in the right direction.

- Don't be concerned if you feel some resistance. Many people find that their internal censor pops up and says, "This is hokey. These affirmations aren't true." If that happens to you, just notice it and do it anyway.

Linda:
Remember my painful thoughts about my daughter? Here they are again with my reframed affirmations:

Initial statements	*Reframed affirmations*
Miah won't have any friends.	Miah has some very good friends. Her friendships are different than mine but no less valuable.
Kids are cruel.	Miah is kind and people recognize that and respond accordingly. In reality, few kids are cruel; in fact, most are nice.
Miah has trouble communicating.	When I listen I understand Miah; she has the skills she needs to make herself understood.
What will Miah's future be like?	Who can see the future? I will love and care for Miah now and the future will take care of itself.

When I find myself worrying about my daughter, I think about my reframed affirmations instead. They help me focus on Miah's strengths and allow me to feel confidence and pride in her abilities.

We'd like to share some other examples of initial statements, revised statements, and reframed statements from other parents in our workshops:

Initial statement:
My son hates me.

Revised statement:
I feel like my son hates me at times because of his aggressive and hostile behavior.

Reframed statement:
My son loves me and trusts me enough to show how badly he is feeling. He knows I will stick by him and love him no matter how he behaves.

Initial statement:
Everything with my daughter is so hard. It takes me an hour and a half just to feed her.

Revised statement:
My daughter's physical needs feel overwhelming to me. I feel like my entire life is consumed with taking care of her.

Reframed statement:
I am so lucky that I am able to be home with her and care for her. I can be sure that she is getting all the love and attention she needs.

(*Linda and Nancy*: We feel that this reframing would also benefit from one addition: "When I need a break, I have competent and loving people who will help me care for her needs." The addition reminds this mom that she is not alone and can call on others when her daughter's needs feel overwhelming.)

Initial statement:
I'm exhausted and resentful because my baby daughter doesn't sleep at night. She has a sleep disorder that keeps her up, and she sleeps only a few hours a night.

Revised statement:
I feel like an awful mother for sleeping while she plays in her crib. It feels like I should be with her.

Reframed statement:
Good mothers need rest. I deserve to sleep and am a better mother for it. My daughter is better served by learning that night-time is for sleeping.

Finally, remember the mom we introduced earlier whose daughter has speech delays? Olivia's mom came up with the following:

Initial statement:
Olivia can't communicate.

Revised statement:
I feel sad that Olivia can't communicate with me verbally because I am missing out on the fullness of communication I would like to have with her.

Reframed statement:
I am doing what I can to help Olivia with her verbal skills. While her skills are developing, I am confident that I am creative and tuned in enough to her to find ways that we can communicate and feel close that don't rely solely on spoken words.

Exercise 4.4: Reframing your painful statements

1. Looking at the Fear/Love chart in Exercise 4.1 and using your reframed statement, brainstorm some ideas about what you might be able to do in the active love quadrant that would help you develop a more useful perspective on this situation. Ask yourself if there is more that you could be doing in the way of educating, advocating, or creating positive solutions. (Often, people find that they are already doing a great deal of active love work and have nothing more to add – that is perfectly all right. In fact, it is important information to recognize and acknowledge.)

   Using the example from Exercise 4.3, you might say:

   - I will continue to make sure Jacob gets the services he needs to maximize his potential.

   - I will investigate independent living options for him as he gets older and it is clearer what type of support he will need.

2. Now, looking at the Fear/Love chart again, brainstorm some ideas about what you might be able to do in the passive love quadrant that would help you develop a more useful and compassionate perspective on this situation. Using the example from Exercise 4.3, some passive love statements might include:

> I trust that we will find the right situation for Jacob and for us when the time comes.

> It's normal to look forward to a relaxing retirement. My resentment about having to worry about this is a human reaction, not a reflection of my feelings about my child.

3. Finally, look for the statements that resonate the most strongly for you and develop a new statement that reflects this perspective. It can be as long or short as you wish. For example, the final reframed statement might look like this:

> We are doing everything we can to ensure that Jacob maximizes his talents and has a full and rewarding life. I am going to focus on what I can do today and trust that we will find good options for him and for us when the time comes to think about his ability to live independently.

4. If time permits, go back and do the same thing for the other two statements you have selected.

Reframing painful situations

Just as we have painful internal thoughts, at times, we also must face painful external situations. Strangers may say things that hurt us or we may have conversations with friends and family that can range from uncomfortable to enraging. The ability to reframe external situations is also a skill we observed in many of the resilient and joyful parents we have met.

A mother of a child with physical disabilities told the following story:

> It really bothered me and my husband that there were some people in our families who never asked about our daughter. They were perfectly aware of the situation yet they never expressed any interest or concern. It really drove us nuts and it was creating a lot of tension. But these were people we cared about so we just decided we were going to tell them about our daughter's health situation whether or not they asked. We said to them, "We understand it can be difficult for you to know what to ask about Amanda, so we thought we'd just give you an update." We did it in a nice way. They generally have been very appreciative that we've taken the initiative to update them – and we feel much better.

By choosing to reframe their family members' "hands off" attitude as discomfort rather than neglect, they were able to find a graceful way to work through an upsetting situation.

In thinking about how we might extend their approach to other types of challenges, we were struck by several things. First, these parents honored their own feelings about the situation without getting stuck in them. They were honest about the fact that this behavior made them feel angry and resentful but they also knew that they didn't want to stay in that emotion. Their strong desire for harmonious family relationships overrode their feelings of resentment and neglect. This positive intention motivated them to proactively address the situation. On our Fear/Love chart, their decision to talk about their daughter's condition openly with their family members is a terrific example of active love.

This couple was also able to see beyond their own emotions and consider what might be motivating their relatives to behave as they did. By doing so, they were able to come up with a solution that met their relatives' discomfort with compassion while making sure their own needs were met. Compassion and acceptance are both aspects of passive love.

And, by choosing a gentle and non-confrontational approach, their relatives had the opportunity to match the parents' energy and intention. In the end, it didn't really matter *why* they didn't inquire about Amanda. Because they were given a generous and face-saving "out", they were able to rise to the occasion and respond with love and concern. Ultimately, that met everyone's needs.

Intentional conversations

It would be great if we always had the time to think through our interactions with others as carefully as Amanda's parents in the previous example. In reality, though, situations often just unfold and we have to be ready to react and respond. Sometimes we're pleased with our responses; other times, we spend the next three days thinking about all the great things we *should* have said.

In our workshop, we often role-play conversations to allow participants the chance to observe and identify where interactions get off track and how we can improve our ability to positively impact the outcomes.

In this role-play, a mother is having an informal meeting about her child's relationships in school. The teacher is clearly frustrated by the child's behavior in class and generally doesn't understand the implications of the child's diagnosis. (We use a fictional diagnosis – visual cerebral functioning or VCF – so that no one in the room will be distracted by listening to the description of the disability more than the interaction.)

> *Conversation One*
>
> *Mom*: Thanks for meeting with me. I wanted to meet because I'm feeling a little concerned about Molly's social relationships with her classmates. She tells me that she often has no one to sit with at lunch or play with at recess. So I'd like to get your perspective about what you are seeing and also what you can do to help her with her social relationships at school.
>
> *Teacher*: Well, I can see that her behavior sometimes is very annoying to her classmates and that's probably the reason she is having problems making friends.
>
> *Mom*: "Annoying" seems like a pretty strong word. What is she doing that is so "annoying"?

Teacher: Well, she frequently interrupts the other kids when they're doing their work and asks them questions that I've just answered. And she gets too close to people and the kids don't like that.

Mom: Did you read the package I gave you at the beginning of the year on Visual Cerebral Functioning (VCF)? The things you are describing are all symptoms of VCF!

Teacher: I did look it over but I can't say I remember all of it. That was the first time I've even heard of VCF. It's one of those new disorders, right? It sounded pretty vague to me. Who told you that she has this problem? Are you sure that this is the real issue? It seems to me that she is really lacking in the social skills area.

Mom: Believe me, we're working with the best doctors in the area and they feel sure that she has pretty severe VCF. In my opinion, a good teacher is one who can help with social skills as well as academic skills by creating a warm supportive environment in the classroom. Don't you agree?

Teacher: Well, yes, of course, but we can't work magic either. Have you thought about maybe a social skills group for her? The local rehab center has some really good ones. Maybe that would be helpful.

Mom: I'm happy to look into that but I'd also really like you to think about what you can do to support Molly socially in the classroom and on the playground. Maybe we could meet again next week to talk about that?

Teacher: Sure. I guess so.

After this brief role-play, we ask the group to comment on what they observed. Usually, they are reasonably complimentary about the mother and very angry with the teacher. They rightly note that the mom kept her cool in a pretty tough situation and that she was successful in getting the teacher to agree to read the information on VCF and to meet again to discuss the mom's concerns.

We then ask the group to focus on the Fear/Love chart in Exercise 4.1 and to reflect on where the mom and the teacher are coming from in this conversation. Using that framework, it becomes easier to see that even with the best of intentions, the mom finds herself pushed into a defensive position that makes it difficult for her to accomplish her real goal of getting support for Molly in her social relationships. She also uses language that pushes the teacher into the fear quadrant of the chart when she suggests that a better teacher would have created a more supportive classroom environment for Molly. The teacher's response ("I can't work miracles") indicates that she was not able to move into the active love quadrant as she deals with her own feelings of frustration with the situation and her underlying concern that she may not have dealt with it fully. Effectively, these two have reached a stalemate in their conversation and very little was accomplished.

We then role-play the conversation again:

Conversation Two

Mom: Thanks for meeting with me. I know the week before winter break can be kind of crazy. But before I get into why I asked to meet with you, I have to tell you that Molly learned so much from the little unit you did on caring for baby animals last month. What a great idea to bring in your kitten to demonstrate some of the things you were teaching. She can't stop talking about how cute the kitten was.

Teacher: That was a lot of fun. Molly was so sweet and gentle with the kitten. She obviously loves animals.

Mom: She does! So, anyway, as I mentioned on the phone, I wanted to do some brainstorming with you on how we can help Molly with her social relationships with her classmates. She tells me that she often has no one to sit with at lunch or play with at recess and I was wondering what you have been observing.

Teacher: Well, I can see that her behavior sometimes is very annoying to her classmates and that's probably the reason she is having problems making friends.

Mom: Can you describe what you are seeing?

Teacher: She frequently interrupts the other kids when they're doing their work and asks them questions that I've just answered. And she gets too close to people and the kids don't like that.

Mom: Oh yes, I've seen her do all those things too. Do you remember the package I gave you at the beginning of the year on VCF? You may not remember the specifics but the things you are describing are very common symptoms of VCF. So, I'm not surprised to hear this. I guess the question is "What can we do to help her?".

Teacher: I did look it over but I can't say I remember all of it. This is the first time I've even heard of VCF. It's one of those new disorders, right? It sounded pretty vague to me. Who told you that she has this problem? Are you sure that this is the real issue? It seems to me that she is really lacking in the social skills area.

Mom: We're working with the best doctors in the area and are confident about the diagnosis. I can give you some additional information if you are interested in learning more about how VCF impacts social functioning. But, for now, please take my word for it that it does. So, do you have any thoughts about how we can help Molly fit in better in the classroom?

Teacher: Well, she needs to work on those behaviors.

Mom: Yes, I totally agree. She is seeing a therapist and those behaviors are under discussion. But I'm wondering what could be done to ease the situation while she is getting those behaviors under control. I had a couple of ideas. Can I throw them out?

Teacher: Of course.

Mom: Well, I was wondering if there are any kids in the class who are particularly compassionate or tolerant. Perhaps someone would be willing to be an occasional helper for her on certain assignments. Or maybe we could consider having the school social worker do a circle of friends for the class?

Teacher: Well, let me think. Cassie is a really sweet little girl who is always helpful. Maybe I could have them sit next to each other in math. And Jenna is often the games organizer at recess. So maybe we could do something with that. Let me think about it. On the circle of friends idea, we recently did something similar for a little boy who was having some difficulties keeping up in PE. Sue, our PE teacher did a very informal circle without singling him out by talking with the whole class about how everyone has things that they are working on and things that come easily and that it is everyone's job to support each other as they work on the things that are a bit more difficult. It was handled so well and the class responded incredibly well.

Mom: That's a great approach. Let me talk with Colleen, the social worker, and see what approach she thinks would be best. I'm open to whatever approach makes the most sense.

Teacher: OK. You know, your comment about the animals also triggered a thought. What if we put Molly in charge of making sure the class guinea pig always has food and water. That would help set her up as a leader in the eyes of the other kids and maybe kids would join her when she is at the cage.

Mom: That's a wonderful idea. Why don't you think about the logistics of that and in the meantime, I'll call Colleen and get her opinion on the circle of friends approach. Can I check back with you on Friday to tell you what she said?

Teacher: Sure. That's fine.

Mom: OK, then. I'll stop by before school starts. Thanks again for your help.

This second conversation has some important differences. First, the mom takes the time to build rapport by sharing some positive feedback on a recent lesson plan. She is also careful to use unifying language, such as "I wanted to do some brainstorming with you", to build a sense of partnership with the teacher. These two decisions signal to the teacher that the conversation is not one where she will feel attacked and this, in turn, puts her in a frame of mind where she is most likely to function from the active love quadrant.

Despite her efforts, however, the teacher's language as she describes Molly's behavior still sounds judgmental. But, rather than becoming defensive, in the second conversation, the mother probes to understand the teacher's perspective and then finds areas of agreement to move the conversation forward in a positive direction. The mother affirms that she has seen these behaviors as well. But once she agrees, she also extends the conversation by connecting the behaviors back to the child's disability. Later in the conversation, she uses the technique again when the teacher attempts to deflect responsibility by suggesting that Molly simply needs to work on her behaviors. The mom agrees and then extends by saying that Molly is working on those behaviors with a therapist but that interim strategies in the classroom are still needed while she gets her behaviors under control.

Her "agree and extend" strategy in both situations again signals the teacher that she does not want the conversation to be confrontational, which makes it easier for the teacher to engage in the real purpose of the conversation – coming up with strategies to help Molly feel more socially at ease in the classroom. The "extend" part of the technique provides a subtle signal to the teacher. It says, "I may be agreeing with you but this is not the end of the conversation. We still have an issue we need to resolve together."

(In some situations true agreement is not possible. However, we can always "acknowledge and extend". Often just letting the other person know that you've heard their perspective can defuse a tense situation. In this case, the mom might have used this approach by saying "I can see her behavior is a cause of stress for you," acknowledging the emotion even if she doesn't agree with the "facts" of the case.)

Another difference in the second conversation is that the mom is very clear about what she is trying to accomplish and does not allow herself be deterred by the teacher's insensitive remarks. This clarity enables her stay in the active love quadrant during the conversation when many people would have given up in frustration and anger.

Her ability to stay in a positive vein also suggests that this mom has done some work in the passive love quadrant prior to the conversation. It's likely that she has accepted the reality that this teacher is not as supportive as she would like and has decided not to let herself get sidetracked by the teacher's attitude.

Many people notice that the teacher's side of the conversation changes very little until the last few minutes. It is true that the mom's skillful handling of the interaction doesn't result in an immediate change. But because the mother comes prepared to propose some specific ideas, she provides a graceful way for the teacher to participate in the solution. It's hard for most people to remain negative when faced with understanding, areas of agreement and concrete positive suggestions.

Exercise 4.5: Improving outcomes of interactions

In this exercise, you will critique and improve a conversation between two parents.

Situation: These two mothers volunteer in their children's classroom on the same day. Mom 1 has a child with learning disabilities and some resulting behavioral challenges. Today was an especially hard day for her son. While she was in the classroom, her son repeatedly interrupted the lesson with off-topic questions and got up from his seat and wandered around the room. Mom 1 noticed the other mother looking at her when her son disrupted the class with what she thought was disapproval. She decides to talk with the mom when their volunteer shifts are over to see if she can provide some context to her son's behavior:

Mom 1: That was a fun math project today. You know, I thought you might be wondering what was going on with Josh today.

Mom 2: Well, I was wondering. He seemed pretty agitated.

Mom 1: Josh has some learning challenges that make it hard for him to focus in class...

Mom 2: (interrupts...) Oh yeah, I know what you mean. Shannon had some learning problems too when she was younger. But we found that really being firm about the homework and clear about our expectations about her behavior in school made a big difference. In less than a year, she went from being behind to being at the top of the class.

Mom 1: We do our best on the homework front but Josh's problems may be a bit more complicated than Shannon's.

Mom 2: Oh, I know. Is he ADHD? But isn't it weird that there seem to be so many kids with all these labels? I don't really remember that when we were young, do you? It seems like it has to do with the schools or the parents. Why would it be so different now? And all the medications...

Mom 1: Well, Josh doesn't have ADHD but his learning problem is related to being unable to process visual and auditory stimulation. He gets really overwhelmed sometimes and things don't make sense to him. Like today for example...

Mom 2: (interrupting again) I think the thing to do is work with him to control himself so that he isn't disrupting the rest of the class. I really sympathize but you can see how hard it is for the rest of the kids and Mrs. Lenox. Have you tried setting up a consequence for him if he doesn't behave in class?

Mom 1: You are assuming he can control his behavior. It's not that simple. I don't want him to feel like he's being punished for something he isn't even doing on purpose.

Mom 2: Well, I'm just trying to help. I just thought that maybe some more structure would help him. I was reading an article the other day about how so many learning disabilities can be handled through better discipline and more structure. But, I don't know.

Maybe you're right. Maybe he's really not cut out to be in a regular classroom.

Mom 1: I didn't say that! You know, let's talk about this another time. I'm running late.

Questions:

1. Where are both moms coming from on the Fear/Love chart?

2. What feelings and reactions do Mom 2's comments trigger in Mom 1?

3. Does Mom 1 accomplish what she set out to accomplish? If not, what prevents her from doing so?

4.   Where in the conversation did things start to go amiss? What could Mom 1 have done differently to change the outcome of this conversation? Go back to the role-play text and write your thoughts in the margins.

There are many different ways this conversation might have come to a happier resolution for Josh's mother. The following version is one example of how this conversation, handled differently, might have led to a more positive outcome:

Mom 1: I thought you might be wondering what was going on with Josh today.

Mom 2: Well, I was wondering. He seemed pretty agitated.

Mom 1: Josh has some learning challenges that make it hard for him to focus in class.

Mom 2: (interrupts…) Oh yeah, I know what you mean. Shannon had some learning problems too when she was younger. But we found that really being firm about the homework and clear about our expectations about her behavior in school really made a big difference. In less than a year, she went from being behind to being at the top of the class.

Mom 1: Wow. That's great. Sounds like that really worked for Shannon. I wish it were so simple for Josh but I think his needs are pretty different from Shannon's.

Mom 2: Oh, I know. Is he ADHD? But isn't it weird that there seem to be so many kids with all these labels? I don't really remember that when we were young, do you? It seems like it has to do with the schools or the parents. Why would it be so different now? And all the medications…

Mom 1: I know. Isn't it amazing how things have progressed from when we were kids? I feel so sorry for those kids we went to school with who had learning or behavior problems and just got labeled the "bad kids" or the "slow kids". Thank God we now know how to diagnose and work with kids on these types of problems. In Josh's case, he doesn't have ADHD but his learning problem is related to being unable to process visual and auditory stimulation. He gets really overwhelmed sometimes and things don't make sense to him. When that happens, he feels really stressed out and looks for ways to relieve his stress – that's why you see him walking around or asking a lot of questions that seem off-topic.

Mom 2: Gee, it's too bad that he's so stressed but I think one of the key things is work with him to control himself so that he isn't disrupting the rest of the class. I really sympathize but you can see how hard it is for the rest of the kids and Mrs. Lenox! Have you tried setting up a consequence for him if he doesn't behave in class?

Mom 1: I don't know that I would call it a consequence-based program but we're definitely working with the school to help redirect him and help him calm himself when he feels stressed. Most days it works pretty well. Today was a hard day, probably because he really struggles with regrouping when the class is working on subtraction. When that happens, I can see how frustrating it is for everyone. I wish it were different but that's where he is right now.

Mom 2: Well, as long as you are working on it… It's just so hard to see the other kids get shortchanged.

Mom 1: Yeah, I can see why you would feel that way. But kids do need to learn that there are people with differences in the world and they also need to learn to be flexible. If you have any ideas about how the other kids might be able to support Josh and help him feel more accepted, I'd love to hear about that. Listen, I've got to run. See you next week.

Exercise 4.6: Reframing a real life situation

In this exercise, think about an actual situation related to your child that was or is upsetting to you. It could be a tense interaction you had with your spouse or a family member, or an unsatisfactory meeting with a teacher.

You may want to focus on a situation that is ongoing or unresolved for you – and where you have the potential to change the outcome by reframing your thoughts and thinking consciously about the interaction that you would like to have.

1. Write a line or two describing the situation. If it helps you to examine the interaction in more detail, feel free to describe it more fully.

2. Looking back at the Fear/Love chart, think about the following:

    • What emotions were motivating the other person or people involved in this situation? Where are they on the Fear/Love chart? Does it change your perspective to try to understand where they were coming from?

    • What emotions governed how you responded to this situation? Where were you on the chart?

3. How satisfied were you with your response (both verbally and emotionally) to this situation? Can you think of a way of reframing the situation that would make you feel better about it? Describe the situation again using the reframing technique.

4. If you had seen the situation the way you just reframed it, how might your real life response have changed? How would the interaction have changed?

5. Now that you have reframed this situation, is there anything you can do to shift the dynamics of this situation or move to a more positive outcome? If this situation is already resolved, can you think of things that you might do differently if faced with a similar situation in the future?

Revisiting past interactions

In our workshops, as people work on this exercise, they often express frustration that they did not handle the situation the way they wish they had. "If only I had thought to say that to him/her at the time!" is a common refrain.

We like to point out that few of us are as eloquent and skilled in the moment as we are afterward in the car driving home and mentally replaying the conversation. But, that's not all bad news. There are some real benefits to reflecting on a conversation and then going back to the person involved for a second go-round. It allows you the space to think about which emotions were motivating (and being triggered by) the conversation, what you wanted to accomplish, and some specific strategies for staying focused on your objective. In many situations, the door is not closed. You can go back to the person in question and say, "I was thinking more about our conversation last week. I don't feel like I really communicated what I wanted to say. Can we try again?"

Giving yourself a little distance from the specific situation can also be an important tool in understanding the other person's point of view. The next story illustrates the power of taking the perspective of the other person. In this story, Karen, the mom of a daughter with cerebral palsy (CP), described her own transformation in dealing with a special education professional in her school district.

> I've been pretty persistent about getting the services I feel that Ellie needs. I guess I'm in his face a lot. One day, though, I started thinking about his job and the stress he must be under not to make the wrong decisions. I realized that he probably worries he'll get fired if he gives in too easily or gives too many services to one kid. It made me feel kind of sorry for him – I know *I* wouldn't want me in my face! After I realized this, my relationship with him really improved. Now we get along really well.

This realization helped move their relationship from one of adversaries to one of partnership. Nothing has really changed in their respective positions – Karen will still push for the best services for her daughter and the special ed professional will still need to balance Karen's needs against the resources of the district – but there is a new sense of mutual respect that makes all the difference in their relationship.

Final thoughts

This chapter introduces the concept of reframing. Some of us are natural "reframers" but many of us need to practice to become truly adept at it. Here are a few final queries to help you integrate the benefits and challenges of reframing:

1. What thoughts emerged as the hardest for you to reframe? Can you identify what makes it hard to let go of those thoughts? Is there something you are gaining by holding onto them? Is what you are gaining by holding onto this thought worth what it is costing you emotionally?

2. Imagine that it is six months from now and you've internalized all your reframed messages. How is your life different now? How do you feel when you look at your child?

Those who do not have the power over the story
that dominates their lives, power to retell it, to
rethink it, deconstruct it, joke about it, and change
it as times change, truly are powerless, because they
cannot think new thoughts.

Salman Rushdie, author, 1991 speech
at Columbia University

CHAPTER 5

Shrinking the Balloon: Seeing Our Child as a Whole Person

The boughs of no two trees ever have the same arrangement. Nature always produces individuals; she never produces classes.

Lydia Maria Child, abolitionist, 1880

Linda:

After Miah was born and for the next few years, it felt like I had this huge balloon in front of my face that kept me from seeing anything besides her label. At first it really wasn't even a balloon, but more like a ball that was so dense I couldn't see anything but her Down syndrome. I remember being in the Target parking lot when she was a baby and wondering if I would *ever* think of anything besides Down syndrome. Over time it has become more translucent, letting light in. Ten years later, it is a small balloon, shrunk tremendously from its original size, hovering in the corner of my mind's eye. I now realize that this balloon is my grief. At first it was so overshadowing I couldn't see anything but pain and loss. Then it was smaller, letting me glimpse around it from time to time, but still in my face on a daily basis. I have worked hard to shrink the balloon and move it to its proper place. I know the balloon will never disappear. In fact, it sometimes blows up to an enormous size, blocking my view again. But the difference is I know it will soon shrink and I have the tools and support needed to allow the balloon to float to its little corner. I also know that the balloon doesn't have to be dreaded. Lots of wisdom and growth have come because of its existence.

The most important tool I have found is seeing my daughter as the beautiful child she is, with many strengths and talents. When I focus on her humanity and giftedness and not her differences and challenges, I relax, enjoying her and motherhood so much more. Her diagnosis, for me, has become like a veil that I used to think was over her face, making seeing her true self somewhat difficult. I now know the veil is actually over my eyes and, though challenging, I have the ability to lift it.

Nancy:
I clearly remember the first time someone suggested to us that Kirsten might have bipolar disorder. After months of trying to solve the mystery of Kirsten's behavior on our own, we consulted a child psychologist and recounted the changes we had seen in the last six months. While she did not presume to diagnose Kirsten on the basis of one conversation with us, she did tell us, "You need to be aware that children with the behaviors you are describing often end up with a diagnosis of bipolar disorder. Kirsten may not have bipolar disorder but it's something to be aware of as a possibility. You may want to start learning more about it."

I felt like someone punched me in the stomach. Bipolar disorder was something I thought I knew something about. When I was 20, I took a year off from college and worked as an aide in an in-patient psychiatric hospital. Over the course of the year, I worked with many patients who entered the hospital in the midst of full-blown manic episodes or in the depths of debilitating depressions. I found both ends of the spectrum frightening and felt great sadness for these patients who were clearly suffering.

And now someone was telling me that my little girl might have this illness. While I couldn't reconcile Kirsten's behavior with my memories of the patients I had known, the mere possibility that she could have the disorder haunted me. I recently read a journal that I kept during this period. In it, I wrote over and over, "She can't be bipolar." Talk about denial. It was almost as if I thought I could ward off the label by refusing to consider it as a possibility.

But ultimately, our growing concern for Kirsten overrode my initial instinct to push this information away. I began to read about the illness and quickly realized the childhood version of bipolar disorder looked nothing like the adult version I had seen in the hospital.

In fact, the more I read, the more I had to admit that Kirsten's behavior sounded very much like the descriptions I was reading of other children with bipolar disorder. Eventually, the three psychiatrists we consulted agreed.

For a long time after that, her diagnosis was all I could focus on. I became obsessed with learning everything I could about early onset bipolar disorder. I read every research study, joined parent list-serves, and tried to master a rudimentary knowledge of brain functioning and the dozens of medications used to treat the illness. If I knew enough, I reasoned, we would be able to figure out how to make this go away. Knowledge was my talisman. I could fix her. She would be my little girl again.

What I initially missed, in all my frenzy to learn everything there was to know about bipolar disorder, was the fact that she still *was* my little girl. Under all those difficult behaviors was my sweet, happy Kirsten still struggling to shine through. Sometimes I work hard to explain this to her. She and I were talking recently after a tough morning. She described herself as a mean person. I replied that I don't think of her as being a mean person but I do think that sometimes she has big feelings that overwhelm her and cause her to behave in ways that aren't the "real her". She looked at me with puzzlement and asked, "But aren't I always me?" "Yes," I agreed. "You are always you. But the things you do or say when you are feeling bad are not who *you* are. You are a wonderful, loving person with a huge heart who has times when you feel very bad. When those feelings come, you have a hard time controlling what you say and do. That's why we are working on helping you figure out other things you can do when you feel bad."

I don't know if I said it well or if she totally understood me. We will no doubt have many variations of this conversation in the future. But, to shrink my balloon, *I* need to hold on to what I told her. She isn't her diagnosis, she isn't her illness. She is Kirsten, my child, a person with strengths and challenges like all of us, and I love her.

Life with a child who has a disability or an illness is a series of adjustments. We often have to adjust our expectations of our child's life, our own parenting experience, and, perhaps, what the future will hold. For some of us, these adjustments begin before our child is born. For others, the adjustments begin at birth or they may not begin until well after birth when a difference or a problem emerges. Whenever we become aware of our child's differences, most of us feel some level of shock, disbelief, and grief as we begin to make adjustments.

We also have different timeframes for finding an explanation for our child's differences. In some situations, the diagnosis is clear and immediate. In many situations, however, we can spend months and even years trying to find the right label that adequately describes our child. Some people *never* find a diagnosis that neatly encompasses the range of their child's needs. Many others make the decision not to seek or use a particular label in identifying their child's differences. But, wherever we ultimately end up on the diagnosis spectrum, it is natural for us to focus on our children's differences, particularly in the early years of dealing with their disability or illness.

Many of our children have needs that will always require a great deal of focus and attention. Nevertheless, we have found that the most joyful and resilient parents are those who are able to "shrink the balloon" and focus on their child as a whole person rather than on their diagnosis or differences. This usually does not happen immediately, but instead comes with time and perspective.

Linda:
When Miah was a toddler and we were in the thick of "early intervention," I was extremely focused on helping her in every possible way. One time I took her to an osteopathic doctor who asked if I *enjoyed* her. Looking back now, I can see that all of my *helping* was actually keeping me from experiencing the joy of being her mother. Our early intervention home teacher, a wise woman who taught me a lot, told me a story that helped me see the importance of *helping* a little less. She had met a man with cerebral palsy who said that he wished his mother had been less focused on fixing him and more focused on letting him have a normal life. When he thought of his childhood, his memories were about therapies. He felt his mother wanted him fixed, and did not accept him for who he was. Later, in college, he was at a bar drinking beer with his buddies. They began to make fun of him by mimicking his unusual speech. He was offended. They pointed out that his speech indeed was difficult to understand. But they *each* had something they all teased about. He was no different. He was truly being accepted and included. *No one expected him to be any different from who he was. He fit in.* Was all my hard

work to help Miah actually more about changing her than helping her be all she could be? Was I accepting her and fostering her sense of self-worth? Or was I giving her the message she needed to change in some way? I'm not saying we shouldn't help our children in any way we can. I am saying we need to examine our intentions and make sure we make our acceptance of them a higher value than their achievement out in the world.

One mom shared her experience of her first year with her daughter with Down syndrome, and how her other 7-year-old daughter helped her put the diagnosis in perspective:

I think for the whole first year, every time I thought of Emily, I thought of Down syndrome. I just couldn't separate the two. I'd think of all the what-ifs. Now when I think about Emily, it's not really about the Down syndrome, it's about all the other things that she does. I don't look at Emily and think "Down syndrome" any more. I think of this little girl who needs help in this area or that area. Like any of my kids.

One of the things that so great about having older kids – my daughter Claire was seven when Emily was born – is how they look at things. One day she said to me, "Mommy, why are you so sad?" I tried to explain to her all the things about Emily that I was sad about. I said, "You know, she might need extra help with things." And Claire said, "Don't all babies need help with things?" I said, "Maybe she'll look different from other people," and Claire said, "Look at us, we all look different from each other." Everything I said she had an answer for, and I thought, "This kid is really amazing." But that's what kids do. They make you see the reality of it.

She went on to describe how her own attitude towards Emily helped other people see her as a whole person as well:

Something that really helped me was the friends who came over and could be normal about Emily. I remember this one time when my friend Mary was over and I was changing Emily's diaper and I said, "Come look at this little baby's toes. They're so cute." Later she said, "At that point, I realized then that I could just treat Emily like a baby." I think everyone was so worried about how to act and what to say but eventually because of how we were with her that everyone just calmed down and realized that she was just a baby. We could play with her. She was a really adorable, joyful baby and her two sisters were all over her all the time. So we eventually came out of that feeling that she should be treated differently.

For many of us, having a diagnosis for our child is a critical part of getting appropriate treatment or therapy. It provides a context for differences and needs and can point us towards the correct medication and therapies if appropriate. At times, however, the diagnosis can become a barrier to experiencing our child as a whole person. At its most negative, the diagnosis can become the basis for stereotyping and limiting thinking.

In his book *The Survivor Personality* (1996), Al Siebert, Ph.D., comments on the danger of over-identifying people with their label:

> It limits understanding. It strips away what is unique about an individual and restricts the mind of the beholder to inaccurate generalizations. A more effective way to view people, and one that allows better understanding, is to assume that every person is more complex, more unpredictable, and more unique than any label. To assume a person is more complex than any theory opens up the possibility that a person can be both one way and the opposite. (p. 31)

One mom we interviewed explained it this way:

> We like to let Jeff be Jeff. The difficult part is the school. We want to let people know that he is not trying to be bad, that he doesn't want power struggles. He can't communicate all of his needs. I think kids with disabilities have a harder time because they don't get away with the typical kid stuff. We want him incorporated into society as much as possible. He also needs to have people around him who accept him for who he is, and don't try to fix him. I don't really believe that he needs to be fixed. Sometimes we like to just goof off. Let him be himself. Sometimes we will go to the creek and throw rocks for two hours. Every time one of us throws a rock, we laugh.

Another mother we interviewed realized she had never done anything alone with her four-year-old son with a hearing loss that didn't involve helping him in some way. In the course of the interview, she realized how different her experience raising him was compared to the experience of raising her other two boys. She vowed to do something weekly with him "that we both just enjoy." She added, "I'm not going to think about giving him a learning experience!"

Letting go of the world's negative perceptions

Though we try to see our children as whole, vital people, the world sometimes does not. How many times have you and your child been stared at by
strangers or has someone talked down to your child? How many times have
you been viewed as either a bad parent or a saint? Most of us try to ignore
the strangers or educate, or set an example. Sometimes we feel impatient,
annoyed, angry, or hurt. Sometimes we can reframe these feelings to recognize that the stranger or acquaintance is just ignorant or curious,
well-meaning but a bit cloddish. The following poem, written by a mother
whose daughter has both physical and cognitive disabilities, sums up quite
eloquently how many of us feel at times advocating for our children, while
remaining whole ourselves.

Metamorphosis

One struggle
Is with identity.
My daughter is her self
And part of our family

With its own unique culture.
But in society
She is perceived
As a child with disabilities and deficits

Who must be "categorized."
This brings us to the "statistic" mentality
That attempts to strip away her
Individual personhood.

As I reject this current,
And buoy her to remain whole,
I, as an individual person
In my own right, get lost

In the maze,
And risk becoming stripped
Of my personhood as well.
I must reclaim
My "self"
And step back in.

Annette Stewart (mother of a child with a disability)

SHRINKING THE BALLOON: SEEING OUR CHILD AS A WHOLE PERSON / 113

Nancy Miller, author of *Nobody's Perfect: Living and Growing with Children Who Have Special Needs* (2002), put it this way:

> If you want your family and friends to be optimistic, you have to lead the way. If you want them to see your child as a total child, you have to be their guide. If you want them to focus on your child's progress, so must you… And remember, nobody's perfect – not even your family and friends. (p. 209)

Another mom with a son with Down syndrome recounted an experience she found troubling:

> When I brought him to pre-school, the first question from the teachers' mouths was, "What is wrong with him?" In my mind there is nothing wrong with him. There is something wrong with people who can't accept diversity. He has a lot of gifts that my typical friends don't have.

She went on to tell this story:

> If people don't get it, I'm not going to spend my time worrying about it. There was a woman who came up to me in the grocery store and said, "Is he a mongoloid?" I said, "Well no, honey, he is from this country!" I thought to myself that I could respond anyway I wanted to. I thought, I don't have to answer. I don't have to look at her. I don't let the negative energy destroy me. I give myself permission to be playful or be serious.

But she went on to tell another story about how perceived insensitivity from others may, at times, turn out to be our own oversensitivity about our children's differences.

> Once, as I was observing my son in karate class, a woman sat down in front of me. I noticed she was looking at him. I was sitting there all mad and I was thinking, "How dare you do that?" She turned to me and said, "Well, that is really strange." I said, "Pardon me?" She responded, "He is the only boy in the class." She wasn't thinking about his disability. She was just thinking that they were all girls except for him.

We have choices as to how we respond to others. The following exercise provides a place to reflect on how best to help our children, ourselves, and others.

Exercise 5.1: Responding to the world

1. What do you tell yourself about other people's looks, questions, or comments about your child? What do you want to tell yourself?

2. How do you want to respond to others who appear to be interested only in your child's difference(s)?

3. Sometimes it helps to have some "canned" responses ready to go when people make various comments or ask certain questions about your child. What comeback comments do you currently use? What else might you say?

4. What do you want to teach other people about your child or about your child's illness or disability?

5. What do you want to teach your child about other people's looks, questions, or comments?

Seeing the world through our child's eyes

One of the ways we can tap into the complexity and uniqueness of each child is by trying to focus on seeing the world through our children's eyes rather than our own. When we are able to look objectively at the lives our children are actually living rather than the one we had hoped they would have, our perspective can change dramatically.

One mom whose 5-year-old son has significant developmental delays explained her philosophy about how she sees her son and how her view differs from that of her ex-husband:

> I think Eric functions very well. I prefer to see the world through Eric's eyes and he is one happy kid. I could put my spin on how Eric *should* be and be sad for all the things he can't do – but Eric is not frustrated and Eric is not sad. Eric is perfectly happy clapping and laughing when someone else does something. It has become about truly looking at the world through Eric's eyes. By contrast, Mark looked at Eric through his own eyes. He would work with him endlessly, he was not embarrassed by him, and he adored him, but he was going to *fix* him. That was the primary difference in our styles.

This mother attributed some of her ability to look at the world through her son's eyes to experiences living in third world countries while she was in college. In processing that experience, she realized that people can and do live full and happy lives that look nothing like our lives – and that many of the things we consider essential for happiness are of much less importance in other parts of the world.

Looking at the world through our child's eyes doesn't always provide us with unmitigated comfort. Sometimes, especially as our children grow older, it is clear that *they* recognize their differences and that these differences cause them pain. But when we acknowledge their pain as valid and real, we are also respecting their wholeness. We are experiencing them as multi-dimensional individuals who have the same range of emotions and the same capacity for joy and sorrow as any other person.

Seeing the world through their eyes also helps us have empathy for our children's perceptions of the world, however different they may be from our own.

> *Nancy:*
> When I interviewed Eric's mom, I was struck by her comments on looking at the world through his eyes. But when I began to think about this idea in the context of Kirsten, I became really sad because it made me aware of how out of control and unfair the world seems to her when she isn't feeling well. I realized that she and I can look at the same situation and see it completely differently but that I often react to her as if she were seeing it the same way I do.
>
> One of our most charged areas of mismatched perceptions has to do with equity and fairness. Kirsten, for example, can be sitting at the breakfast table with a huge stack of pancakes in front of her and become extremely upset because "Molly has more pancakes!" Typically I would look at Molly's plate – which generally has far less food – and point out to Kirsten that she already has more than Molly.
>
> Looking at this recurring situation through *my* eyes, it is easy for me to fall into judging her behavior as irrational, inflexible, and greedy. But, when I look at the situation through her eyes, I can see that she feels overwhelmed by intense feelings of deprivation and jealousy that have nothing to do with the number of pancakes on her plate. She is telling me, "I don't feel loved enough right now. I'm afraid I'll never have enough." Instead of judging her or trying to

talk her out of her feelings, I try to remember to say something like, "You feel like Molly has more food than you do. What can we do to make it feel fairer?" If she wants another pancake, I give it to her. After all, who cares if we waste a pancake or two if she ends up feeling understood and supported? I wish that it were always this simple to make things feel "fair". Sometimes her feelings are so huge there is no immediate fix. But when I concentrate on seeing the world through her eyes, it helps me move from a place of anger and frustration to one of empathy and compassion.

Exercise 5.2: Looking at the world through your child's eyes

1. Think about the world as your child sees it. What adjectives would you use to describe his or her view of the world?

2. How do you think your child would describe his or her life to a stranger? What would they say is wonderful about it? What would they say is difficult?

3. Go through a stack of old magazines and tear out any picture that speaks to you about how your child sees their world. Create a collage that captures some of the feelings you described earlier. Or, using paints, crayons or any other materials that appeal to you, create a picture that represents these feelings.

4. Did thinking about the world through your child's eyes bring up any feelings or thoughts for you? Describe any shifts in your emotions or attitudes when you think about the world from his or her perspective.

Examining our own expectations

Sometimes the power of our own dreams and expectations for our children can make it very hard to "shrink the balloon" as quickly as we might like. An athletic dad who dreams of coaching his son's soccer team may feel great pain when his child's disability precludes his participation in certain team sports. A mom who values academic achievement highly may find her child's cognitive impairments very difficult to accept. We may find that aspects of our own lives we have valued the most – our friendships, academic or professional success, children, athletic accomplishments – are the areas that trigger our deepest feelings of grief when we imagine our children's future.

Initially, all we may be able to see is that our children will not be able to have the life that we dreamed for them and, by extension, that *we* will not have the life we dreamed for ourselves. This is a completely normal reaction in the face of loss. It would take a pretty unusual person to give up certain long-cherished dreams and expectations and feel genuine excitement about their child's new possibilities. The process of letting go of old dreams and building new ones takes time.

Many parents find that their feelings of loss do not follow a defined or predictable path that leads to a sense of resolution and peace. Even after many years of living with the loss of an old dream, feelings of grief can pop up unexpectedly. For example, the mother who thinks that she has successfully resolved her feelings of sadness about her child's cognitive impairment might be surprised at the intensity of her feelings of loss during her child's late teen years as her friends' children begin to apply to colleges and make plans to leave home. A parent who highly values social acceptance may feel wretched on the night of the senior prom if her child cannot participate. Old dreams often die hard.

We all have our areas of pain. Developing new dreams does not completely eliminate the old dreams but it does make their loss easier to bear. Often we hear from parents that the old dreams don't go away but are re-interpreted in the light of the child's abilities. As one mother of a son with cerebral palsy commented, "At first it seemed like our dreams were gone but now I can see that they don't have to be gone – they're just different."

Linda:
Before Miah was born, I imagined all the things we would do together – hiking, sharing life stories, taking her to college, and planning a wedding were just a few. I was afraid that none of these dreams would come to be until I found myself watching her dance a solo at an outdoor creek festival. There she was – poised, graceful, confident, and happy. I realized this wasn't in my fantasy of her before she was born. It was better. The truth is I don't know what the future holds. I may not help her plan a wedding – *or I might*. Now the dream is about her finding her own way – her own source of happiness and fulfillment. I am giving her opportunities to find those sources and I am giving myself the freedom to dream old dreams as well as new ones. For me, the only important dream is of her experiencing joy – and *joy* can take many different forms.

Sometimes parents find that living with a child with special needs has the unexpected benefit of putting things in perspective for them.

One mother, whose youngest daughter has Down syndrome, had the following comments on watching her typical oldest daughter's friends apply to colleges.

My oldest daughter is a junior in high school and is starting to think about colleges. It amazes me how crazy the parents around here are getting about the whole thing. For me, it's just such a non-issue. I just want my daughter to pick a school where she thinks she will be happy. From living with Sarah, I know that that is the only thing that matters. It puts it all in perspective. Having your children happy and healthy, that's what counts. The rest is all icing on the cake.

Another mom of a son with autism commented:

> I don't take things for granted. I know some other parents who get almost sick of hearing their kids say "I love you" because they say it so often. It's like they go, "Yeah, yeah, I love you, too." But for me, the day my son told me he loved me was the best present I ever received. We appreciate things on a different level. I can see now that he's going to be his own special person.

Finally, a mom of a baby with Down syndrome expressed her feelings as follows:

> I'm really lucky. Dean is such a sweet guy. He's been such a blessing from the start. Even his heart issues were a blessing in a way. All I wanted was for him to be healthy. It really put the Down syndrome in perspective. I guess I've found that joy comes in unexpected little pieces, not in big chunks.

Appreciating what is and focusing on strengths

When the balloon starts to shrink, the whole person comes into focus. Our children's illness or disability becomes one aspect of who they are – often something significant – but it does not *define* them. It becomes as natural to focus on their strengths as it does on their differences. When this shift takes place, many parents feel a deep sense of appreciation for their children's unique qualities.

This mom of a pre-schooler with developmental disabilities shared the following story:

> I vacillate back and forth between limiting Sam by thinking, "Okay. He'll be able to ride the bus, have a menial job, have friends, and things like that." But then he says something that makes me feel that I've underestimated him. For example, he likes to carry around a meat tenderizer (he calls it a meat cleaver). I have no idea why. Usually I discourage him from taking it outside the house since most people think it's pretty odd! But once we were going to the library and he wanted to bring it. He said to me, "Mommy, meat cleaver is heavy." I agreed with him. Then he said, "But meat cleaver isn't dangerous. Heavy can go to the library but dangerous can't go to the library!" And that kind of stuff still brings me up short. I feel like he gives us a perspective that we wouldn't have. He grounds all of us. I think he has something special. He looks at the world differently, which causes everyone around him to slow down and stop. He says,

"Mommy, I'm not hurrying. We're going to walk really, really slow."
So you walk really, really slow and you see a few things.

The mother of a daughter with a developmental disability expressed her awareness and appreciation of her daughter's gifts as follows:

> I try to let people see Liza's strengths because our society is so focused on intelligence, so focused on being able to do what other people can do. People don't see what Liza *can* do that other people *can't.* I see it now but I didn't in the beginning. It has taken me some time to see how gifted she is in certain areas. They aren't always areas valued by society. She is very gifted spiritually. She has a connection and knows what is going on the "other side". She is also gifted musically. She is able to move with music and feel it in her body and relate to it even when she doesn't understand all the words. She is in touch with other people. Last year she went to a camp with people with special needs. She cared about the people who were in wheelchairs. She wanted to know more about them. She has a strong intuition about people, especially about which people feel safe and which people need a hug. She likes to learn. She has an incredible amount of determination. She will work really hard.

Another mother of a son with language and social developmental delays found that she has come full circle from fearing her child's differences to cherishing his unique perspective and gifts:

> At this point for me, I have shifted hugely from wanting him to be "typical" to a sense of great excitement for his gifts and talents. This is a kid who really excites me because he has mysterious, bright, raw creativity. He's not very affected by social conventions. You might say that he's free in a way. Earlier I hid his differences and I didn't want to talk about them. I still don't talk about them all that much, but at the same time I am not hiding... We all have individual ways of learning. I've come to the conclusion that uniqueness is a fine thing and often a source of beauty. I have made fabulous friends because of Jamie. I have met so many wonderful families. I feel very enriched by that. I feel like I have expanded my compassion towards human beings about differences. I am at a place where I feel lucky.

In Klein and Schive's book *You Will Dream New Dreams* (2001), the mother of a child with Down syndrome summed up her feelings about her son's challenges in the following passage:

My son *has* Down's syndrome. It soon became a statement of fact. He *has* blond hair; he *has* blue eyes; he *has* Down's syndrome.

Yes, the Down's syndrome has presented a challenge to us as parents determined to help him develop to his fullest potential. But aren't all parents similarly challenged? Don't we all want each of our children to develop to his or her fullest potential?

The differences lie in the way each child is challenged and, sometimes, in the timing – when and how the challenge is presented. My son's challenge was conveniently bundled up and labeled for us immediately, present from the moment of his conception. Almost from the start, we knew what we were dealing with.

And over time, I came to realize that our child was more like typical children than not, that life holds no guarantees for anyone, and that life's very unpredictable nature is what makes it so special. That what we truly love about each child is his or her *uniqueness*, not that which makes them just like every other child.

My love for him is complete, and his Down's syndrome has become an inseparable part of that love, just as it is an inseparable part of him. I am very proud of all that he had accomplished, and I take nothing for granted. I look forward to discovering what his future holds. (p. 76)

This natural sense of appreciation can be cultivated by make a point of focusing on the positives. One mom of a son whose behaviors can make her day very trying shared a practice that has made a difference in her life.

Every night before I go to sleep, I write down at least one thing that went well that day with Ryan. Even if it has been a horrible day and I have to write down something like, "He didn't break anything today," *I find something* positive to say. That helps me end the day thinking good thoughts about him.

Exercise 5.4: Focusing on strengths: good parent messages

In his book *Body, Self, and Soul: Sustaining Integration* (1992), Jack Rosenberg identified a set of core messages that his research determined we all need to hear from our parents to be whole, healthy, vital human beings. These messages include statements such as "I love you," "you are special to me," "I'll be there for you," "I give you permission to be different from me," and "it's not what you do, it's who you are that I love."

In this exercise, we are going to think about the additional messages our children need to hear in order to feel whole.

1. What messages did you receive as a child? Were any important messages missing?

2. How do you communicate positive messages to your child? Would you like to add more messages? Is something missing from the messages you're communicating?

3. What can you do to communicate these messages non-verbally?

4. What message does your child need most? (Choose from Rosenberg's list or contribute one of your own.)

5. What were you taught about disability and/or mental illness? What messages are you giving your child about these conditions? Are these the messages you want to be giving?

Now that you've completed these exercises, we'd like to share some of the messages that parents in our workshop came up with for their children:

- I'm proud of you.
- You are a blessing to me.
- You are stronger than you think.
- You make me happy.
- I love being with you.
- You are not your behavior.
- You are a part of me.
- I'll never leave you.
- You are not your diagnosis/disability.
- I love being your mother/father.
- I'm lucky to have you.

One mom commented, "I want to hang these messages up on my wall and look at them every day. If I could focus on these feelings instead of the negatives, it would really change how I interact with my son."

We also need to remember to give *ourselves* appropriate messages. We like this message from Kate Divine McAnaney's book, *I Wish... Dreams and Realities of Parenting a Special Needs Child* (1998). She writes "Today, I will remember that my perspective is different from my child's. I'll remember not to get caught up in grieving on his behalf. I will focus on what my child can do and will help him set reasonable goals." (p. 12)

Exercise 5.5: Focusing on strengths: a letter to your child

1. Write a letter to your child describing him or her. Imagine you are feeling your most loving, positive, and strong. Feel free to gush. Tell your child who he or she is in your eyes. What do you love about him? What are your dreams for her? Say as much or as little as you want to about their illness or disability.

2. Add a paragraph about the parent you hope to be and the relationship you want to have with your child. Write this in the present tense.

3. If you like, rewrite this letter on a separate piece of paper and put it away to share with your child at a future date.

Questions:

1. How would your relationship with your child change if you
    were able to feel these loving, positive feelings about him or her
    all the time?

2. What can you do to reinforce these feelings about your child?

Celebration

One of the wonderful ways resilient parents focus on their children's
strengths is by finding ways to celebrate their children's milestones and
accomplishments. This is particularly important in families where the
child's condition has taken them off the chart of typical developmental
milestones. The family has a chance to recognize and celebrate the child's
progress on their own timeline, whenever it occurs.

Celebration becomes a family matter and a source of joy for everyone.
One mom of a son with global developmental delays commented, "Milestones have gotten smaller but more important and more significant. I
remember the day he crawled. The whole family was cheering for him."

Celebrations don't always have to be a big deal to be meaningful to us
and our kids. They can be a heartfelt "I'm proud of you," a special call to a
grandparent or a friend to share positive news, or a high-five that says, "You
did it!"

Linda:

For me, celebrating Miah's successes has not only been important in our everyday life, but has also been an important part of her therapies. I don't ever want her to feel she is not "good enough" or that therapy isn't fun even though it's also work. This value became crystal clear for me when Miah was just a baby. We were at an occupational therapy appointment and I expressed great excitement and hope that she would crawl soon. She was on all fours doing that preliminary rocking movement and she just seemed ready to me. The therapist informed me that it would be months before she would crawl. That week she began to crawl! I was elated and arrived at the next O.T. appointment ready to celebrate, but instead of encouraging Miah to crawl and us to clap, the therapist had her work on fine motor skills. I didn't say anything at the time, but now I make sure the professionals working with Miah value a job well done and allow her (and me) to relish it instead of rushing on to the next skill to be mastered.

Another father explained how his family celebrates:

Blake loves parties. We will go out sometimes to celebrate. We will do it to make a big deal about his doing something. He feels proud and we feel proud. Life is more fun when you stop a minute to appreciate it.

And another mother with a daughter with motor issues summed up her feelings of gratitude as follows:

We hang up Julie's work on the refrigerator and that kind of thing. We do it to celebrate and encourage her. She takes a gymnastics class and her brothers sat and clapped for her after she did an entire reenactment. She couldn't jump forward and she showed us one day she could. We were all so proud of her because she worked really hard to do that.

She went on to describe her gratitude for her daughter's gifts:

I hate the expression "Your child must be such a blessing," because I think it is very judgmental, like all my kids aren't "blessings". And yet there are such extraordinary gifts that come, and you don't know what they are going to be in the beginning. You just know that they are going to come. When you are having a baby, your job is to love the baby and figure out what the baby's gifts are.

Exercise 5.6: Celebrating our children's achievements and milestones

1. Describe some of the ways your family has celebrated your child's strengths and achievements.

2. What else can you do to express your honest delight in your child's accomplishments? What would be especially meaningful to your child?

3. What are your child's gifts? What has been your child's biggest gift to you?

Final thoughts

This chapter is about the important shift in our mindset that takes place when we can see and appreciate our children as the unique and loveable individuals they are. When we are seeing them in their totality, their strengths become evident and their challenges are seen in perspective. We allow ourselves to feel the pain associated with the loss of our old dreams but we find ways to create new dreams. We understand that the new dreams are not a consolation prize; they *are* different from the old dreams but they are wonderful in their own right. When this happens, our children grow and blossom and we can embrace them for who they are, not who we expected them to be.

The next exercise is a meditation to help us visualize our children as the people they are. You might want to practice this often, thinking of your child with all of his or her gifts.

Exercise 5.7: Meditation

- Sit in a comfortable position. Relax completely. Breathe deeply.

- Visualize a light within your heart – glowing radiantly and warmly. Feel it radiating larger and larger. Feel it radiating love all around you.

- Stay with this until you have a strong sense of your energy being filled with pure, unconditional love.

- Now envision your child. See him or her radiating pure love. Name all the gifts he or she has to offer. Now send your loving energy to your child. See him or her embraced by it.

Now see your child send his or her loving energy back to you. Feel this connection of love and appreciation. Thank your child for all he or she has given you. Listen as he or she thanks you in return.

One last story

One woman shared the following story about her mother, who was instrumental in helping the family create a way to celebrate the accomplishments of her son who has cerebral palsy. We were moved by the grandmother's sensitivity to her daughter's sadness as well as the way she communicated her own positive expectations for her grandson's growth and development.

> Soon after Jackson was just born, I was at a baby shower for a healthy, typical, perfect baby. Someone gave the baby one of those milestone calendars. I felt so sad. After the shower, I said to my mother, "Jackson will never have one of those." She never forgot that. So every year for the last 15 years, my mom has bought Jackson a calendar for his birthday and we record every milestone we can

think of in it. For example, 2½ weeks ago he swallowed a pill whole for the first time. We celebrated and it went on the calendar.

Everything in life that we really accept undergoes a change. So suffering must become love. That is the mystery.

Katherine Mansfield (1927, p.165)

CHAPTER 6

Building Our Children's Village: Deepening Our Child's Connections to Others

It takes a village to raise a child.

African proverb

Hillary Clinton popularized the African proverb that "it takes a village to raise a child" in her book of the same title several years ago. While we love the image of the village, sometimes we feel that if it takes a village to raise a typically developing child, then it takes an entire city to raise ours! Our discussions with parents in interviews and workshops support this notion. We have found that the most joyful and resilient parents are those who don't try to go it alone. They are skilled at forming, cultivating, and celebrating their children's connections to other people.

The ability to build a village – which we define as a supportive, caring community – for our children includes the capacity to identify and develop relationships with people who have the willingness to form deep bonds with our children. It also requires that we create enough space in our lives to enable these relationships to take root and flourish and that we trust others enough to allow them to play a meaningful role in our children's lives.

Building a community for our children is important on several fronts. For many of us, caring for our kids, no matter how much we adore them, is an exhausting and all-consuming commitment. In order to care for ourselves and to have the emotional and physical vitality to build a joyful life, we need other people in our lives to help and support our children. Having a village allows us to enjoy time away from our children without guilt or worry, knowing that they are in good hands.

Nancy:

I recently met with Kirsten's therapist. She is a wonderful woman; warm, empathetic and wise. John and I believe she is doing all the right stuff with Kirsten. Yet all three of us have had to admit that concrete evidence of Kirsten's progress has been limited. With that in mind, I asked her therapist if she felt it made sense to continue working with Kirsten.

She said that she had also been thinking about that question and admitted that she'd had to significantly scale back her own short-term expectations of "progress" since beginning her work with Kirsten.

But then she went on to say something that has stayed with me, especially in writing this chapter. She said that even though it *has* been hard to see progress with Kirsten, she believes there is value in staying the course. She commented, "I see myself as a consistent person in Kirsten's life who is regularly checking in with her and is there to help her reflect on how she is doing and what she is feeling. Even with her ups and downs, our relationship will be something she can count on. In addition to supporting Kirsten, I hope I can be an outlet for you and John. This is a very difficult situation. You need people who can be containers for some of your feelings – people to whom you can say *anything* and know that it's OK."

Her comments articulated the value of having other people in our lives who are deeply involved with our children. John and I are fortunate to have a number of such people in our lives. We have designated this special group the honorary members of "Team Kirsten". From babysitters to professionals to family members and close friends, we have created a community that shares a commitment to seeing Kirsten do well and seeing our family thrive. We are grateful to every member of the team for how they support her *and* us. Our lives are immeasurably richer because of them.

Linda:

"You'll attract more bees with honey than you will with vinegar" is an old saying I've tried to take to heart when dealing with people who are involved with my daughter. It's not that I'm sugary sweet or dishonest; in fact, I've given some feedback that I'm sure service providers haven't always wanted to hear. But they have been able to hear it because we had already established an open, trusting relationship. How? By setting the stage beforehand. And I do this by acknowledging what they were doing right and letting them know they are appreciated. I've found that people will walk the extra mile for my family when they feel valued. A heartfelt thank-you note, munchies at an IEP meeting, and letters to supervisors about an employee for a job well done go a long way with professionals who are often undervalued.

I once asked a professional to please use person-first language (e.g. referring to Miah as a child with Down syndrome rather than as a Down syndrome child) when talking to me about Miah. I explained how much we respected and valued her work and how I had not always used person-first language myself (I didn't even know what it was before Miah was a baby though I worked as a school psychologist!). Though I was nervous about broaching this subject with the professional beforehand, our "emotional bank account" was filled enough that she not only heard me, but embraced my request and had the *entire* university's speech and language department do the same.

Having a variety of people in Miah's life has helped create a joyful life for her. Miah has different kinds of support in different kinds of places. Remember when I talked about her friendships in the early elementary years and how difficult that was? The lifesavers were friends from several other arenas of her life. The church youth choir welcomed her every Wednesday afternoon. When she felt left out at school, she asked for Paige, our neighbor, to come over. She danced a solo in an intergenerational, inclusive dance troupe, and enjoyed one-on-one time with friends of the family. All these special people made what might have been a pretty awful couple of years for her self-esteem and my sanity fairly positive. She learned that support comes from many places and I learned that peace comes from casting a wide net.

Like us, our children also benefit enormously from having other committed people in their lives. The presence of these supporters reinforces that they are important to a broad community and builds their sense of security and self-esteem. These relationships also provide them with opportunities to interact with a variety of people which in turn enables them to develop the flexibility they need to adapt successfully to different situations.

Building a village for our children obviously makes good sense for everyone. But how does it come about?

Sometimes, it just happens on its own. We are blessed when we have people in our lives who are there for us and our children in deep and sustained ways. Often these are close friends and family members or a trusted group of talented professionals.

Beyond this special group, however, lies the rest of the world. As one mom put it, "How can you tell who is willing to be involved with your child?"

Many people we know who are good at creating community for their children do it quite automatically, never stopping to analyze what they are doing. When we step back from our personal experience and our many conversations with parents, however, we can see that there is an underlying set of skills that supports the formation of these important relationships.

These skills include:

- using our intuition to identify potential supporters
- putting out feelers to test the waters
- cultivating relationships and expressing appreciation
- clear communication about our child's situation and needs
- trusting others to take care of our children.

Identifying potential supporters

Many of the people who are invested in our kids have a reason to be. They are close relatives or caring professionals who work with our children. But sometimes, we find pockets of support in unexpected places and people.

Linda:
I am blessed with many friends. I never thought that some of them would also be my daughter's friends until I received a call one day from a wonderful woman who goes to my church. She asked if Miah could attend *Godspell* at a dinner theatre with her and a group from church. At first, I thought the invitation was for both of us, and, since I didn't really want to go, I declined. But she explained that the invitation was for *Miah*, though I was welcome to come as well. Hmm. Sure… Great! Miah went to the play, had a fabulous time, and many in the group commented on how much they enjoyed

having her along. I feel such comfort in knowing there are many adults out there who will enjoy her if given the opportunity.

Nancy:

Kirsten's Brownie troop leader Robin was awesome about making sure Kirsten always felt included as a full member of the troop. Due to her high standards for her Brownies, she always made sure that girls in the troop treated each other with respect and consideration. Even when Kirsten was taking a break from active involvement in the troop, she checked in regularly with us to make sure that Kirsten was aware of all the troop activities. Her message to us was consistent: Kirsten is a member of our troop and we love to have her join us. We always knew that Kirsten would be not only safe, but well cared for at Brownies. We were grateful to Robin for always making the extra effort when it would be so easy to let Kirsten drift away from the group.

One beautiful story we heard about cultivating unexpected supporters came from a mom whose son has Fragile X, a genetic disorder that affects physical and cognitive development. This boy's disabilities have made friendships challenging and limit his opportunities to interact with a wide variety of people. That hasn't stopped his creative and resourceful mother, however. Her ability to recognize people with generous, caring spirits has helped her son build ongoing relationships with two people who are in his life on a regular basis – the mailman and the produce manager at their local supermarket. Both men regularly take time out of their busy workdays to connect with her child, to interact with him and include him in their daily routines. Her son's relationship with these men infuses otherwise ordinary events such as the mail drop or a trip to the market with a sense of fun, community, and friendship.

Another wonderful example of an unexpected source of support is the following story of a girl with significant learning differences and her horse. Her mother explained:

Her horseback riding has been a godsend because it is the only place she feels just like everyone else. She has a terrific teacher who loves her and she works out a lot of life's struggles with her horse.

Exercise 6.1: Identifying potential fellow villagers

Who are the current and potential supporters in your life? Sometimes we just feel a caring energy from people. Other people may have had life experiences that make them more open or compassionate toward children with special needs. They may go out of their way to include your child or to make you feel welcome at a gathering. As one mom put it, "I look for people who treat my child like a person and not like they are being 'nice' to a poor disabled child."

The purpose of this exercise is to help you think about your child's current and potential supporters.

1. Write down the names of the people that you include in your child's village. Next to each person's name, write down what you remember about how that relationship between your child and that person began.

2. Who else would you like to see become part of your child's village? What is it about makes you want to include these people on this list? What makes them special? Why do you want these relationships to develop?

Testing the waters

Once we've identified who we would like to have in our children's lives, we often need to put out feelers to see how people will respond. While the potential pay-off is huge, this can sometimes feel like a risky step.

One mom we interviewed, Sarah, shared a poignant story about her attempts to elicit support for another child. Sarah had a friend whose child, like her own, has significant developmental delays. This little girl was starting pre-school for the first time and her mother shared her concerns about her daughter's adjustment to this new situation with Sarah. A week or so after her conversation with her friend, Sarah ran into a couple she knew whose daughter, Emma, attended the same pre-school. Excitedly she told them all about her friend and her daughter and suggested that perhaps Emma could take this child under her wing and help her make the transition to the pre-school. In our conversation Sarah said:

> When I finally slowed down, I saw that the husband of the couple was looking at me like I was crazy. It was obvious that he didn't want his daughter put in the role of helper and didn't want her to have to deal with "that sort of thing." I was mortified.

> I don't know how you figure out who the supportive parents are and tap into them. I guess I get afraid – if they really don't want anything to do with my child, I need to know that. I need to know not to bug them about it or approach them.

She went on to contrast this father's attitude with her own when her older daughter was in pre-school.

> When my girls were little they went to an inclusive pre-school. It truly made my daughter much more compassionate and understanding. When she had information about other kids' differences, she was very understanding. One little boy in her class had a brain injury – his frustration threshold was really, really low and he would just go off. But Max was one of her best buddies. She said, "You know, when Max gets really frustrated, Mommy, I run." She understood that this was part of Max and that you just needed to get out of the way when it happened. And I thought it was great. I thought it was awesome that she was able to do that.

While Sarah's experience with the other parents was disappointing, she, in fact, provided the answer to her own question by testing the waters – in this case by attempting to enlist a family's support for her friend's child. Yes, there is a risk that we may get a negative reaction, but there is an even great potential for people to delight us with their willingness to engage and connect. In many cases, we simply cannot know until we try.

Exercise 6.2: Testing the waters

Many of us are understandably afraid of rejection – and the sting can be even more painful when it feels like it is directed at our child. Yet, in many situations, we need to make the first move if the relationship is going to move forward. This exercise will help you think about testing the waters with some of your potential "villagers".

1. Think about the people who you identified in Exercise 6.1 as potential supporters of your child. For each person, brainstorm and write down some ideas of ways that you can test the waters.

   Would it be a deeper conversation about your child or yourself? Would you be comfortable asking for their help or support? Is there something that you could do that might be helpful to them? Would you like to invite their child over for a play date? Try to be as specific as possible when you think of your own ideas and match the idea to the particular person.

2. Select at least two people on your list whom you would feel comfortable approaching to test the waters. Set a goal for yourself of contacting these people (or more!) in the next month.

Deepening the relationships

Once we've identified people with the spirit and willingness to enter into a relationship with our child, the next opportunity to build our child's village is to find genuine and honest ways to deepen those relationships.

Ann and Rudd Turnbull, authors of many books on families and disability, have developed a list of suggestions for professional's who work with families. While their recommendations focus on professionals, several are also great suggestions for families who want to strengthen relationships with professionals and other supporters in our children's lives.

Their list includes the following:

- Know yourself – understand how you perceive the world and how your perceptions differ from those of others. What are your values? Are they the same as those of the professionals who work with your child?

- Know the people in your child's life – don't judge them and don't assume you understand all the dynamics involved in their relationships. People are complex.

- If people don't agree with you, try to understand their points of view.

- Build on people's strengths: all of us do better when affirmed and not put down.

- Communicate positively (treat others as you would like to be treated).

- Be worthy of trust and respect.

(Adapted from Turnbull and Turnbull 2001)

Everyone who touches your lives will have a different relationship with your child. Some are wonderful playmates, others are great for initiating outings, still others are wonderful at cuddling, listening and understanding. As you expand your community, reflect on how you can build on each person's strengths, fostering the natural evolution of the relationship and affirming each person's unique contributions to your child's community.

Linda:
Miah's kindergarten teacher was very competent but didn't quite seem to click with Miah on a personal level. Instead of focusing on what wasn't working so well, Mark and I decided to focus on her

strength as a teacher and hired her as a tutor for Miah one afternoon a week. We wanted the extra academic support for Miah but we also wanted the teacher to get to know Miah better as a person. The teacher ended up becoming very close to Miah and was a terrific support to her and us for the rest of the year.

Nancy:

The value of recognizing and appreciating different people's strengths crystallized for me when we were on vacation in New England a few years ago. Shortly after we arrived, Kirsten's medications stopped working and she was irritable, filled with rage, and very difficult for most of the vacation. Because we were visiting many different friends in a 10-day period, I was able to see and appreciate their wonderful range of skills in dealing with this stressful situation. My friend Gail's infectious sense of fun helped to distract Kirsten from her misery. Suzanne, a proactive and skilled problem solver, helped us think about how we could head off problems by developing alternatives to our initial plans that minimized stress for Kirsten and the rest of us. Laurie wasn't always sure how to help Kirsten but she held me and comforted me when I cried. Each friend's contribution was a natural outgrowth of her own personality and strengths. It really brought home the fact that different people support us in different ways.

Exercise 6.3: Recognizing others' strengths

1. Next to the names of the people on your "supporters" list, write down what it is that you value most about each person's relationship with your child. What natural strengths does each supporter bring to the relationship?

2. What could you do to foster the natural connection that has been started with your child?

3. Brainstorm other ways that you could help bring more joyfulness and emotional attachment to the individuals and groups who interact with your child.

Expressing appreciation

One of the most powerful ways we know to deepen relationships is to express our appreciation of the other person. Being appreciated is not only wonderful for the person who is being recognized – it also makes us feel great to make them happy.

Nancy:
Kirsten was very fortunate to have a wonderful second grade teacher. Mrs. Cox had incredible experience and skills from her many years as a special ed teacher before moving to a typical classroom. One of the things John and I admired was her wonderful, almost matter of fact attitude about kids and their needs. She understood that *every* child has different needs and that her job as a teacher was to work with the kids wherever they were, whether they were grade levels ahead or behind. She also displayed a willingness to communicate with us on a flexible and frequent basis through conferences, email, daily contacts, and snippets of conversation in

the halls. Best of all, she never made us feel that we were bothering her or taking up too much of her time.

When Christmas came, we wanted to show our appreciation. Around the same time, I read an article in which several teachers were queried about their favorite holiday remembrances. While they all agreed that gifts are nice, they were unanimous in saying that a heart-felt card or something made by the child was the most meaningful gift of all. So, along with our tray of baked goodies, we made a special card for Mrs. Cox. On one side was a note from us telling her how much we appreciated her efforts on Kirsten's behalf. On the other side was a picture of Kirsten sitting on Santa's lap along with a special note from Kirsten saying that she had asked Santa for the best teacher in the world and had gotten Mrs. Cox. Kirsten came home glowing and reported that Mrs. Cox said she would keep her card forever. We were pleased. Knowing Mrs. Cox, we were sure she had found a way to make each child feel very special.

A few months later, a student teacher named Courtney joined the classroom. She too was wonderful and we quickly approached her about tutoring Kirsten after school (always trying to build that community!) In the course of our conversation, she told us that one of the first things Mrs. Cox had shown her was our Christmas card. She commented to Courtney, "This is why we teach. It's so great when you can make a difference and people appreciate it." I had hoped that our card would be special to her and it felt wonderful to find out that it was. It made me appreciate her even more.

Linda:

One year, there was a little boy in Miah's class who had some special needs. His parents were very unhappy with the teacher and complained to the principal about her. In the end, they wrote a letter expressing their feelings about the teacher for her personnel file. There was so much distrust and hostility between the teacher and parents that they couldn't sit in the same room comfortably. We had been nothing but pleased with this teacher and felt very badly that she was ending up with a black mark on her record. Mark wrote a letter for her file expressing our confidence in her and our deep appreciation of the skill she had displayed in working with Miah. She was very grateful that we made this extra effort and it helped solidify her already strong relationship with us and with Miah to know that we appreciated her efforts. Though on occasion it's necessary to do battle on behalf of your child, I've found that working to form partnerships and creating mutual respect is more likely to benefit everyone.

For many of us, an important part of appreciation is giving back. One mother of a child with bipolar disorder described a dear friend who has been a huge source of support for her daughter.

> When Kayla ran away, my friend spent countless hours helping us try to locate her. After we found her, she stayed with my friend for several weeks. Even now that she is back home, my friend drives her to her weekly therapy sessions. I know that I can't ever repay her for all she has done for us but I try to express my appreciation in a lot of little ways. I do things for her, buy her little gifts that I know she'll like. I want her to know how much she has helped us.

Exercise 6.4: Deepening relationships and appreciating your supporters

1. Think about the people you identified in Exercise 6.1 who are already involved with your child. What can you do to help deepen those relationships?

2. What could you do to show your appreciation for these people? Going person by person, brainstorm what each might especially enjoy.

3. Write a note to someone you want to appreciate. Now get a piece of stationery, copy the note, and mail it!

Getting others to see our children as individuals

In spite of the negative reaction she got from the father of the typical child, Sarah, the mom who advocated for her friend's child, is both skilled and resourceful at building her own child's village. One of her great strengths is her ability to get others to see her son as an individual and not just a diagnosis or a collection of problems. We love this story of how she cracked a hard nut – an insurance company claims adjuster – and got her to see her son as a person who needed the insurance company's help and support.

> Brian's speech therapy got turned down by insurance and I decided to fight it on principle. There was a woman I talked to a bunch of times and I worked to make Brian very human for her. I compared him to her son – her son was getting speech therapy at school and I asked her why he was receiving those services. She said he had a speech impediment. So I explained that my son could barely communicate verbally at that time. It took him off a piece of paper and made him real to her. She could imagine what it would be like if her child could not communicate. And that was huge. I think for the most part people are caring. So, if you look at that, you say, "OK, how can I get you to understand?"
>
> I have a friend who has two kids with ADHD. They are also very bright. But they can be hard kids to like sometimes, due to their behavior. I tell my friend, "Karen, just find one thing that the teachers can relate to about the kids." For example, one of them is a really talented artist. Once you find that thing, that area of mutual interest or of an adult's appreciation for a child's talent, it opens a door to empathy for that child.

Open communications

Getting others to see our children as individuals means that we must be able to talk about our children and their situations openly and honestly with others. Without appropriate information, others may not understand what is going on with our children. Sarah shared a valuable story that makes this point:

> I was once part of a home-schooling group. There was an interesting situation with one mother. Her 10-year-old son had some kind of severe behavioral and sensory integration issues, but she never explained that to anybody in the group. He participated in several different group activities, but he had no consideration for other kids' personal space. This was really hard for some of the kids. Another mother in the group, after two years of making comments to this woman about how her son's behaviors were affecting her own child, ended up pulling her son out of the group and starting another program. Well, when the first mom found out about it, she wrote a very hateful email about how her son wasn't being included and how the other mom had made an unfair judgment call. I thought that was unfair on her part because she had never enlightened the other woman about her son's issues and challenges.

It's easy to see how a lack of information – particularly in situations where children have no apparent physical differences – can contribute to misperceptions and/or harsh judgments about our kids. Yet, deciding who to tell and how much to tell can be a complicated decision for many parents.

One mom of a pre-school daughter with Down syndrome shared her philosophy:

> I have a small group of people I tell everything to. All the little things that hurt me, Cassidy's most extreme behaviors, all my painful thoughts. But this group is very limited. I prefer not to share everything with most people, even friends, because I don't want those things to be in their minds when they look at Cassidy and interact with her. I want them to focus on her strengths and the things that make her special. And, I don't want their pity. I trust my small group of "A Team" friends to be able to listen to me and understand me without feeling sorry for me.

This mother is able to distinguish between when she shares information about her child with others because *she* needs support and understanding and when she is sharing information to help her child. She recognizes that certain information can influence how others see her daughter and she is selective about where and when she shares that information.

Many parents find that as they are more able to accept their child's challenges, it is easier and more natural to communicate openly about them with others. One mother of a son with language and social developmental delays described the shift in her attitude in the following way:

> I used to really worry about what people thought. For example, when we were interviewing babysitters or checking out homecare or pre-schools, I would want to explain *a lot* about my son's issues, but I was afraid that they would reject him and us. In fact, I discovered that too much information wasn't always a good strategy. Finding the right balance was key. Now I am at the point where I just think, '"This is just information about him and our family and I shouldn't be afraid to share it. What is the big deal? If it is a big deal for you, then you are not our new babysitter or this isn't the right place for my child."

Sometimes we may feel resistance to the idea of talking about our child's illness or disability with others. There can be a variety of reasons for this reluctance. These discussions may feel like an invasion of our privacy or our children's privacy. It may feel overwhelming to have to educate people about our child's needs. We may fear being misunderstood. Sometimes the resistance may come from a fear of being judged or pitied. Other times, it just doesn't feel worth the effort.

All these feelings are valid and there are undoubtedly times when it makes sense to honor them. When these feelings prevent us from openly communicating with people who form our child's community, however, it is worthwhile to explore our feelings of resistance more closely. Many times we find that our internal "scripts" are making the communication more emotionally loaded and difficult than it needs to be.

Nancy:
Unlike parents of children with visible disabilities, I have always had a choice about what I told the world about Kirsten's situation. I could say nothing and allow them to draw their own conclusions. I could chalk up some of her behaviors to unspecified issues or a bad phase. Or I could talk about her behaviors in the context of her

illness. Every situation with a new person required a decision about what I would say or not say.

When she was first diagnosed with bipolar disorder, I found it wrenching to talk about her diagnosis with most people. At first I told myself that this was appropriate since I didn't want her to suffer from the stigma that our society puts on mental illness. Gradually, though, I came to realize that my reticence was as much – or more – about my own feelings about mental illness as it was about my perceptions of societal attitudes. *I* was ashamed and uncomfortable. Her diagnosis felt like a secret that I had to keep from the world.

Ultimately, the burden of keeping the secret became too great and the reasons for communicating more openly became more compelling. John and I decided to send a letter to close family and friends in which we "officially" told people about Kirsten's diagnosis and gave them detailed information about early onset bipolar disorder and its impact on Kirsten's life. This first step set the stage for more honest communication with this important group of people in our lives.

Yet, even after I grew more comfortable in talking about her illness, I continued to struggle with the fear that I was violating her privacy. These fears were piqued when Linda and I were asked to give the keynote speech for an agency fundraiser. The prospect of talking about Kirsten's diagnosis in front of 300 people kept me up for several nights. Finally, after much discussion, John asked me the following question: "How would you like Kirsten to feel about her illness?" I thought for a moment and said, "I would like her to feel matter of fact about it. That everyone has differences and challenges and this one is hers. I want her to be puzzled about why anyone would ever make a big deal about it."

Once I said that, it was clear to me that if I wanted *her* to feel that way, I needed to model feeling that way myself. This one realization has set the tone for my communications. Now, when I do decide to tell people about Kirsten's illness, I try to be as matter of fact as possible. I don't communicate tragedy or self-pity. I simply tell the people who need to know. I'm still pretty selective about who is included in that group but I no longer feel so reluctant to talk about her diagnosis. It's made a big difference to my comfort and confidence in dealing with her illness and I believe it will make a big difference to her down the road.

Linda:

When Miah had attended kindergarten for a couple of months, it became obvious that the other children needed some explanation of why she was the way she was. I prepared a great talk and even had a friend who is a filmmaker make a short video about Miah and her non-school friends. It was well received by the kids and I believe it helped Miah. I, however, felt terrible! I went to my car and wept. It was hard to have to explain my daughter. I talked to her class this year, and again it was well received. I think it helped her have her best school year yet! However, it was not nearly as difficult for me. Why? More acceptance and practice on my part. I still wish that *none* of us ever had to explain our children. But until that day arrives, offering information with compassion and sensitivity is usually helpful.

Exercise 6.5: Working through resistance

1. When you think about talking about your child with any of the people on your lists, do you notice any feelings of resistance? A good first step is to clarify all the reasons why you *want* to communicate more openly with others about your child. Write down your thoughts on what you would gain from this communication. What would the benefits be for yourself and your child?

2. Next, write down all the negative consequences you can imagine resulting from inadequate communications about your child. What do you stand to lose?

3. If you feel resistance to talking about your child's disability or illness, write down your uncomfortable thoughts about these potential discussions. Try to identify what emotions these thoughts are triggering.

4. Using the techniques introduced in Chapter 4, reframe these uncomfortable thoughts into more positive statements. For example, "I'm afraid that she will withdraw from us if she knows that Jason has Asperger's syndrome" could become "This conversation will give her the information she needs to understand Jason's behavior. Her reaction will give me the information I need to understand if she is able to compassionately deal with his differences."

5. Notice if these uncomfortable thoughts are general or if they are centered on a particular person. If they are related to a particular person, try to identify why. What information are you getting from your feelings about this person? Is this an opportunity to reframe your perceptions? Or is it your intuition asking you to look more closely at whether this is someone whose support you want to cultivate?

Exercise 6.6: Preparing your "script"

Making conscious decisions about what you want to share about your child's disability or illness is both appropriate and respectful of your feelings and your child's feelings. In this exercise, we are going to work on articulating what we want to share and with whom.

1. Looking back again on Exercise 6.1, write down the names of each person you feel will be a valuable addition to your child's life. By each person's name, jot down how much information he or she currently has about your child's situation. (Try a simple rating system such as "too much, enough, some, little, none" or whatever else works for you.)

2. Place a star next to the names of the people you feel do not have sufficient information about your child.

3. Make a list of things you could do to further educate the people on this list. Try to include a range of possibilities, from sharing factual information to a more detailed personal conversation. You could gather some resources together to help with the information sharing. This would be a great opportunity to compile a list of favorite websites, articles, books, and other resources so that you have them all in one place.

4. Go back to your list and see which of these resources or other strategies is appropriate and comfortable for you to share with the people whose names you starred. Identify at least three actions that you could comfortably take in the next month.

Trusting others and letting go

The final skill in building our child's village is our own ability to let go enough to allow other people the opportunity to develop independent relationships with our children. Like most parents, we know our children intimately and can read their needs and their moods better than anyone else. But for many of us, the intensity of our children's needs has honed this parental instinct into an art form. We can tell at a glance when our children are tired, anxious, or stressed. What's more, we often know exactly which response or approach will be the most helpful at any given moment.

It can be difficult to think about entrusting the emotional or physical well being of our children to people less experienced at reading and responding to them. Our minds churn out endless scenarios of things that could go wrong, from behavioral issues ("what if she has a tantrum?") to medical emergencies ("what if he has a seizure?").

We do not mean to minimize anyone's feelings about letting go. It *is* painful to imagine our child needing us and not being there to smooth rough waters. We also may fear that our children's behavior or needs will be a turn-off to the people who are caring for them and we want to protect them from any judgment or disapproval. But, hard as it may be, letting go is necessary both for our own respite and for our child to develop and mature.

The mother of a son with autism summed up her increased ability to let go as follows:

> I used to worry about having other people take care of Justin. I would spend the whole time wondering if he was throwing a fit or smearing poop all over. Then I finally realized that anyone I would trust to take care of him already knew he might do these things. They weren't worried about it, so why should I be? It wasn't the end of the world if he wasn't perfect for them.

Another parent with a daughter with articulation difficulties and motor issues described how she wants to advocate for her child:

> I used to say that my job was to speak for my child, but that is not true because it is about me helping her speak for herself. That is taking *me* out of it in a way. I am the midwife. A good midwife is almost invisible in the room. Even though I am not that quiet right now, I am going to have to go into kindergarten and talk to the school about Lidia and talk to the parents. I want to make it completely up front for everyone. I want everyone to just talk about it. Then I won't have to do it every day. I am going to get this started and then I am going to back off.

By this point you have created a plan to further cultivate your child's support system. Now you will need to step aside and allow others and your child to create magic. Some people might call this process "putting it into God's hands." Whatever you call it, most of us need faith – faith in others, faith in our child, faith in the universe. We have planted the seeds, yet it is important to realize we cannot make them grow.

How do we know when we need to let go a little? Maybe it's when we find ourselves in a constant state of worry and paralysis. Maybe it's when we feel so tied to a particular outcome that that we see no room for other possibilities.

These feelings can be clues that it is time to step back and surrender some of our deeply held beliefs. We can surrender the belief that we must always *fight* for our children. Sometimes it is appropriate to fight, but this is rare. We can surrender the notion that things have to be painful and dramatic. We can surrender the "us against the world" mindset in favor of collaboration and partnership.

We can plan and set the stage for our children and their relationships, but trying to control them will only get in the way. Once we've let go, we may be amazed by the wonderful opportunities and people waiting for our children.

Exercise 6.7: Reframing our expectations of our child and others

This exercise is often helpful for people with younger children who are not yet fully "out in the world".

1. We all have various beliefs about how children "should" behave
    or function in order to be a valued member of a community.
    Write down three beliefs that you have about how your child
    needs to behave or the abilities he or she needs to have in order
    to be accepted in the world (e.g. "my child should be polite" or
    "my child should be potty trained").

2. Reframe your beliefs to reflect more positive and open
    expectations of your child. ("It's OK if Sean isn't polite all the
    time; no child is" or "the people that I would trust to take care
    of Laurel already know she isn't potty trained so it's not an issue
    for them".)

3. How would your feelings about having others care for your
    child shift if you knew that they shared these more relaxed
    expectations of your child?

4. We also have certain beliefs about our community of supporters
    and how they interact with our children. What beliefs do you
    hold about your supporters? Write down three beliefs or
    expectations you have about people who support you and your
    child (e.g. "They should always feel positively about being with
    my child" or "They need to follow the same routines with my
    child as I do").

5. Reframe these beliefs to shift your expectations of your supporters to a more accepting mindset (e.g. "It's OK if Susie doesn't always have positive feelings about being with Ian – I don't always have positive feelings myself!" or "It's healthy for Ian to get used to doing things differently than I do. I'm helping him become more flexible").

6. Would you be more likely to allow others to care for your child if you could internalize these reframed expectations?

7. If anxiety about trusting others is getting in your way, some general affirmations may help you feel more confident and secure. Develop three general affirmations that remind you that you want to be trusting and confident with your supporters (e.g. "I don't have to control this. I can relax. I can allow this relationship to unfold").

8. Make a collage, paint or draw a scene in which your child is loving life with others. Don't include yourself in the scene. Use this space to let go and enjoy thinking of your child's relationships with others.

9. Write every negative thought you have about why your child can't have the life he or she deserves on a separate sheet of paper. Roll it in a ball and throw it in the garbage, remembering that thoughts are just thoughts and not *truths*.

This chapter has focused on building a village of support for your child. We've seen that identifying supporters, testing the waters, deepening relationships, expressing appreciation, opening communication, and trusting others are all essential to building your child's community.

Exercise 6.8: Final thoughts

1. Of all the skills discussed in this chapter, which do you feel are natural strengths for you? Which are the most challenging? What makes them challenging?

2. Imagine that you have a group of trusted supporters who are deeply committed to your child's well being. What would feel different about your own life if this village was in place?

Like the body that is made up of different limbs and organs, all mortal creatures exist depending on one another.

Hindu proverb

CHAPTER 7

Knocking on the Door:
Building Our Support Systems

Ask, and it will be given to you: seek and you will
find; knock and the door will be opened to you.
For everyone who asks, receives; and
everyone who seeks, finds; and for everyone
who knocks, the door will be opened.

(Matthew 7:7–8, New Revised Standard Version)

Nancy:

An important part of my self-image is my perception that I am a good friend, someone who is there for others when the chips are down. Over the years, I've had many opportunities to listen to my friends' problems and I've been glad to provide whatever assistance I can. Yet, until Kirsten's illness, I didn't have much experience in asking others to do the same for me. I consider myself to be extremely lucky to have many wonderful friends as well as caring, supportive parents who live close by. Still, the idea of asking people to help me was very difficult and foreign to me. I tended to wait passively for people to offer assistance or express empathy about our situation. I confess I felt great resentment when that didn't happen as frequently or consistently as I would have liked. I found myself thinking, "Where is everybody now that *I* need some help and support?"

One day I was talking with my therapist about a dear friend who lives 2,000 miles away. I was expressing my sadness and anger that she had barely been in touch while we were going through such a terrible time. My therapist (a very practical woman) asked me a simple question: "What could your friend do that would be helpful to you?" I thought about that and replied, "I just want to know that she cares and is thinking about us on a regular basis. An email or a phone call once a month would be great." My therapist said, "That seems pretty reasonable. Why don't you ask her to do that?"

After stifling an impulse to tell my therapist that she was over-simplifying the situation, I had to agree that her suggestion was a pretty straightforward solution to my feelings of neglect. She went on to say, "She may not be able to do it. But if she can't, that's infor-mation for you also. At least you will know." What a liberating thought for me! I could just ask someone to do something and if they were not able to do it, I could see it as information rather than a blatant rejection.

Looking back on the conversation, I am amazed that I didn't come up with this idea on my own. Yet, it genuinely didn't occur to me to simply think about what would be helpful and ask for it. Nor did it occur to me that I wouldn't drop dead of disappointment and humiliation if the person didn't come through for me.

I went home and emailed my friend. She responded immedi-ately. She expressed regret that I had to ask her to do something so basic for me and promised to do better in the future. And do you know what? She has. That simple, obvious piece of advice salvaged a 30-year-old friendship that is very dear to me.

Have I completely internalized my therapist's advice in my own life? Not fully. I still find it hard to ask for help for myself, but at least now I remember the two simple steps: think about what would help and ask for it.

Linda:
The day my sister died was one of the hardest days of my life. I grieved deeply for her child, our mother, our whole family, but mostly, I grieved for myself. Miah was three and our second daughter was about to be born. My sister was my A#1 supporter. Who was going to take care of Miah while I gave birth? In fact, who would take care of Miah years from now when the rest of the family wanted to hike some mountain and Miah couldn't keep up? My sister listened to the details of my life: my grief about my daughter's situation, my anger at friends who didn't seem to get it, and my pride in her abilities. Who would share my joy, my pain? My

husband loves me deeply and is supportive, but he is *in* it with me. I sometimes needed someone a bit more removed.

It's been seven years since her death and I've made a point to develop other "sisterly" relationships. At first, I talked about my feelings about Miah more and more to a trustworthy friend who has no children and loves me and mine. She is now the girls' guardian should anything ever happen to Mark and me. Then I enlarged my circle to include other mothers with kids with differences. One woman has a child with a seizure disorder, another a child with language and social issues, and another a child with a developmental disability. It didn't matter what the difference was, just that they "got it" and were the type of people I would choose to be friends with because of who they are. This circle has grown. It has become a huge source of support and encouragement, and a major vehicle for growth for us all.

Three years ago several of us started meeting to brainstorm ideas for issues our kids were facing. We asked to use a room one night a week at the pre-school our children attended. These meetings were the beginning of something *big* for me. One mom attended a workshop put on by a dance therapist, loved it, and suggested we hire her to lead our group. We invited other women we respected and thought would like such a format (including one woman who did not have a child with special needs, but who just seemed like a good fit). We meet once a month to explore our personal journeys, our mothering, our joys and challenges. When I think of how our group has evolved over these three years, I'm amazed! In the beginning, it was mostly about mothering our kids with differences and now it's about *us* – our struggles, our dreams. Oh, we touch on issues with our children when the need arises, but time and our trust in one another have enabled us to stretch in deep, heartfelt ways. What direction do we want our lives to go in? How do we expand our relationships with our partners? What patterns are we stuck in that we'd like to shift?

I am grateful to have women in my life I can call, say "let's go for a hike," and tell all those important life stories to. They listen well, offer support, and sometimes challenge me. Being able to talk about my feelings, no matter how difficult, is crucial if I want to work through my fears and hurt. Acceptance of my situation comes from being honest, heard and loved.

In the last chapter, we stressed that the ability to create a circle of invested supporters for your child is a critical element of building a joyful life and is an important hallmark of resilient parents.

But what about asking for help for ourselves? Ah. That, it turns out, is a whole different ball of wax. In our workshops, we have people work on an exercise that you can do in this chapter. It's Exercise 7.3: Building your circles of support. In this exercise, we ask parents to write the names of intimates, friends and supporters within three concentric circles. Next, you are asked to identify specific things you would be willing to ask these people to do to offer you tangible forms of help. But here's the catch. You should identify things that would be helpful to *you*, not your child.

To be honest, when we created this exercise, we thought it would be relatively straightforward and easy for parents. After all, most of the parents in our workshops are extremely skilled at finding resources for their children and are appropriately assertive – even aggressive – about asking for help for them. Therefore, we were surprised by the intensity of emotion this exercise unleashed. We found that even the act of *thinking* about asking for help turned out to be among the most emotionally charged areas we have explored with parents.

What makes this exercise so difficult for many people?

For starters, most of us, especially women, are used to being the helpers, not the "helpees". Asking for help can make us feel vulnerable and needy. For many people, these feelings are more of a challenge than the problem we need help with. "I don't want people feeling sorry for me" is a common refrain that we hear from parents. This exercise can trigger all of those feelings. In this chapter, we'll explore how to reframe the belief that asking for help equals weakness. We will also explore our concern that we are opening ourselves up to emotional vulnerability or rejection.

The exercise also makes some people aware of how little they are able to ask for help in virtually any situation. One woman shared a moving anecdote that exemplified this problem. A week or so before our workshop, we had a major snowstorm. Susan related that she had been unable to leave her condo for three days because her car was completely snowed in and she did not own a shovel. With tears in her eyes, she told the group, "I couldn't even go next door and ask my neighbor if I could borrow his shovel." As a single mom of a teenager with significant mental health issues, Susan had built her self-image and public persona around being completely self-sufficient and independent. Can you imagine how difficult it was for Susan to come up with specific favors she could ask of the people in her circles of support?

Other people re-lived the pain they felt on the occasions when they did ask for help but it was not forthcoming. Many people concluded (usually on the basis of relatively few negative experiences) that help would never be available or reliable and that it is easier not to ask. The stories we tell ourselves about why people do or do not help play a huge role in our willingness to put ourselves out there again.

For still others, the exercise triggered feelings of great loss or emptiness. One woman wept throughout the exercise thinking about the death of a beloved sibling and the recent move of another friend, both of whom had been key members of her "intimates" circle. Another woman shared with great pain that she felt she had no one but her husband to put in her intimates circle. She felt that she had pushed everyone in her life away because of her "obsession" with her son's problems. "I don't have a social life. I don't have any friends," she commented. For her, the exercise compounded her feelings of loneliness and isolation.

Finally, for others, this exercise brought up feelings of guilt that they are imposing on the lives of their friends and family by asking for or accepting help.

Once we understood many of the thoughts and feelings behind asking for help, it became easy to see why this exercise brought up intense emotions for many people. We began to realize that getting people to ask for and accept help requires much more than simply listing ways other people can help. We must also address the underlying feelings.

Exercise 7.1: Examining our assumptions about asking for help

This exercise is designed to help you look at some of the messages you internalized while growing up as well as your current beliefs about asking for help.

1. What were you taught as a child, either through words or by example, about asking for help? How do you feel this influenced you?

2. What were you taught about giving help?

3. What are your worst fears about asking others for help?

4. Select two fears that are most painful and real to you and try to reframe them by rewriting them using the framework from Chapter 4.

    • *Fear 1*
    Initial statement:

    Reframed statement:

- *Fear 2*
  Initial statement:

  Reframed statement:

Exercise 7.2: What would help you?

In this exercise, we want you to think about everything that the people in your life could do to be helpful to you. Many people have trouble articulating what would be helpful to them. So, when people ask, "What can I do to help?" many of us choke and say, "I can't think of anything." The purpose of this exercise is to help you have a few specific items on your list so that when people ask you what they can do, you have some ready answers. It is also a necessary step to prepare for Exercise 7.3.

Here are a few tips about getting the most out of this exercise.

- Remember that you are trying to come up with things that would be helpful to *you*, not your child. (Of course, feel free to include things that are also helpful to your child – such as a friend taking him for a play date – but make sure the primary focus is on you and your needs.)

- Go back to your energy pies from Chapter 2 and see where you said you wanted to make some changes in your life. Think about what people could do to help you free up some energy for those changes.

- Don't edit yourself. Write down everything from your biggest wishes ("I wish someone would send me on a two-week vacation to Hawaii") to your smallest wishes. Even if something seems unobtainable right now, feel free to write it down anyway.

- Acknowledge your first thought – which might be "I can't do anything unless someone takes my child" – and stretch beyond it. Respite *is* critically important. But it's only one of many things people can do to help. Be as creative and specific as you can be to get the most out of this exercise.

Questions:

1. What can others do to support you emotionally? Call you? Send you a funny card? Tell you that you are a great parent? Come over and watch the basketball game with you? Bring you an ice cream sundae? What would make you feel great?

2. What can others do to help you with the practical realities of life?

For example, a friend of ours has a friend whose child has CP. Because she lives far away from her friend, she knows that providing respite care is not feasible. On her annual visits, however, she noticed that her friend's dryer had broken and that she did not seem to have the time or resources to get it fixed. So, as a gift, our friend ordered a new dryer for her friend. Her comment was, "I wanted to do something to make her life a little easier and this seemed like a practical way to do that."

We may not all have the means to offer such a generous gift, but our friend's impulse to help is accessible to all of us on whatever scale fits our lives and those of the people in our circles. What can people you know do to help you deal with the "wet laundry" of your life?

3.   What can others do to support your life goals and objectives? Be as out there as you want.

Exercise 7.3: Building your circles of support

Now that we've identified specific ways that others can help you, this exercise is designed to help you think about the people who comprise your circles of support.

1.   Think about all of the people important to your life and write their names within different rings of the circle. The people to whom you are closest should inhabit the innermost ring (intimates), your second closest group should inhabit the next ring out (friends), and your third group should go in the outer ring (supporters).

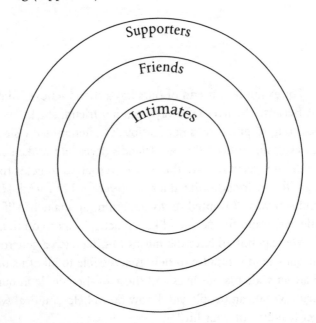

Figure 7.1: Circles of support

2. As you are filling in your circle, consider the following:

- family members

- friends

- neighbors

- people with whom you work or volunteer

- people in your religious or spiritual community

- members of groups or organizations

- online friends (many support groups are now "virtual").

3. Next, put a star next to the people in your three circles who you feel are in a position to be helpful to you and are likely to respond positively if you ask them to help.

4. Go back to your previous list of "asks" and look at the things you identified that would be helpful to you. Now look at your circle, and identify one person in each ring whom you would feel comfortable approaching about your requests. Looking at your top ten list, keep on matching your "ask" to the appropriate people until you have matched each request with a person in your circles.

Getting past negative experiences of asking for help

One of the things that can make it difficult for us to ask for help is our previous experiences of asking for help. Every one of us, no matter how loved and cherished by friends and family, has had the experience of asking for help and not receiving the support we need. Perhaps it was that neighbor who has said, "Call me if you ever want me to take Sean," but never seems to be able to do it when you call. Or that little edge in your sister's voice when you ask if she can pick up the food for your parents' anniversary party because your daughter is having a hard day. ("Wait a minute," you say to yourself. "Isn't she the one who is always asking me what she can do to help?") Whatever your example, it's likely that you have felt let down at some point.

Unfortunately, because it *is* so hard to ask, these experiences can completely shut down the asker – and not just with the person who let us down but with almost everybody.

Here are some of the thoughts that run through our heads when we feel let down.

- People say that they are going to help but they never do.

- No one will be there for me.

- No one cares about me (or my child).

- Everyone is completely wrapped up in their own life.

- It's easier just to do it myself.

- I can't count on anyone.

- I'd rather not impose.

Recognize any of these? Whether we say them aloud to ourselves or not, most of us have little pieces of these thoughts stuck in our brains somewhere. This is where reframing is an essential tool.

Let's go back to our example of the grudging conversation with your sister. She agrees to pick up the food for the party but clearly isn't pleased about it. You can tell yourself something like this: "She says she wants to help but when I ask her to do the simplest thing, she acts like it's a big deal. I'm never asking her to help me again."

But, depending on your relationship with her and your previous experiences with her, other stories are possible:

> Boy, she sounded stressed. It's too bad that I had to ask her when she's having a rough day but she did say that she wanted to help. I'm going to assume she meant it even if she sounds a little put out.

or

> I forget how stressful these family parties are for Lynn because of her tense relationship with Mom. Maybe I can distract Mom at the party so she doesn't focus on Lynn and grill her about her job search.

You get the idea. There may be a gamut of other things that could be affecting the other person's reaction to your request that have nothing to do with you, your child, or even the request itself. In truth, we often don't know what is going on with the other person unless we ask.

So, now it's your turn to try reframing a situation.

Exercise 7.4: Reframing a disappointing interaction

1. Write about a situation where you asked someone for help and they let you down in some way.

2. What did you tell yourself about the situation?

3. What other interpretations might you have made about this situation?

4. Choose one that feels the most plausible. Reframe your initial story using this interpretation instead.

5. Imagine that you are having a conversation with this person about the situation. What do you want to ask them? What would be helpful to know in terms of setting realistic expectations for the future?

On occasion, in all of our lives, we run across someone we care about who truly is unable or unwilling to help. It may feel like the person is unreliable or unsupportive. It hurts and you feel angry and resentful. This is where the "it's all information" mindset can really help you. Keep in mind that it is unlikely that this person's behavior is any reflection on you.

Imagine the following situation. You have a friend who is aware of your child's situation but never inquires about him or her or offers to help in any way. You've tried in a variety of ways to get this person to be more supportive – talking about your feelings, asking for specific support – but nothing has made a difference.

An appropriate reframing of the situation might be something like this:

Initial statement:
Julie never asks about Justin and never offers to help. It's obvious she doesn't care about us enough to help us when we're in great need. Who needs "friends" like this?

Reframed statement:
For whatever reason, Julie has not been a support to me around Justin's needs and is not likely to be in the future. This isn't a reflection of me or Justin. It's a reflection of who Julie is as a person. There are other things I do like about Julie and I can choose to focus on those if I decide that I want to continue this relationship.

The reframed statement does several things. First, it states the truth in a factual way – Julie has *not* been a help and that fact is not likely to change. But it avoids making the next leap, the one that makes me feel horrible: "She doesn't care about us enough to help us when we are in great need." In fact, I don't know that Julie doesn't care about us enough. Given that I still consider her a friend, this is most likely not a true statement.

This reframed statement also avoids self-blame. This is Julie's issue. There are many reasons why people don't or can't reach out to others in their time of need. We may not know *why* they can't but it isn't our fault or a reflection of our worth as people.

Finally, it introduces an important element of choice. You may decide that if Julie can't be there for you when you really need her, you don't want to continue the friendship. Or, if there are enough other things that work in the relationship, you may decide that you do want to continue the friendship but will accept that Julie is unlikely to offer tangible help or support to your family. In either event, it's your decision and you make it with your eyes open.

Can you imagine how much less emotional energy it would take to think about Julie in this way? Suddenly, you are back in the driver's seat with this relationship. You have moved from being a victim (the person Julie doesn't care about enough) to being in control (you understand her limitations and can choose to accept them or not).

Try reframing one of these relationships yourself by thinking about a situation where you needed or asked for help but didn't get your needs met.

Building your inner circle

We mentioned at the beginning of the chapter that the circles of support exercise makes some people sad because they realize that they have very few people in their intimate and/or friends circle. There are many reasons why this may be so but none of them make the reality any less painful. While we have no magic fix for this situation, we can offer the following thoughts:

- Recognize that, with the exception of family members, few people in our lives start out in the inner circle. Usually, our inner circle intimates begin as more casual relationships that then deepen over time. To cultivate your inner circle, you usually need to start with your outer circles. This may involve investing in relationships in your "friends" or "supporters" circle in a more concerted way or it may involve bringing new people into your life.

- Reread the section in Chapter 6 on cultivating relationships with people who will become invested in your child's well being. The same principles apply to finding people who will support you.

- Connect with other parents who are dealing with similar situations. This can be a formal support group or simply an individual or two. Knowing that you are not alone can be a tremendous source of support and relief.

- Select at least one activity that interests you that involves other people and make sure you are including it in your life on a regular basis. It is really helpful to try to expand your relationships with people based on something other than your child. Perhaps it's a book club, scrap-booking, a biking club – whatever will get you out and doing something you truly enjoy.

- Examine some of your thoughts about the people in your life. Can you reframe your perceptions with the goal of finding a deeper way to include these people in your life?

- Keep working on all aspects of building a joyful life. The better you are able to put your feelings about your child's disability or illness in perspective, the more energy you will have for reaching out to other people and building satisfying relationships.

Exercise 7.5: Creating a supportive group for yourself

If you are not in a supportive group and would like to be in one, we strongly encourage you to join one or create one. This exercise will help get your creative juices flowing so you can visualize what you are looking for.

1. Dusty Miller, in her book, *Your Surviving Spirit* (2003), talks about the importance of being part of a community for strengthening our internal resources.

   What do you think of when you think of a loving and compassionate community of support? Think about the people and organizations/groups in your life that make you feel accepted and nurtured. If nothing comes to mind, write about the kind of support network you would like to cultivate.

2. Make a list of the three groups or individuals with whom you would like to deepen your connection:

   (a)

   (b)

   (c)

3. List at least one thing you could do to deepen each of these three connections.

    (a)

    (b)

    (c)

Getting past "I don't like to impose"

To ask for and accept help, we must get past the idea that we are imposing on others. Or rather, we must get past the idea that people necessarily mind being imposed on! We can all think of times when someone we cared about was in need and we were delighted to lend a hand. In fact, we probably didn't think of it as being "imposed on" at all. We were just happy to be helpful in that situation.

Many of us, however, put our own situation in another bucket. Usually it's not a crisis situation – the death, the unexpected hospitalization – that we need help with. It is the daily ongoing challenge of life with our special kids that can be exhausting. And because of the ongoing nature of our challenges, it's easy to assume that people will grow tired of being asked for their assistance. In our experience, however, this is generally not the case.

Carol Staudacher, author of *A Time to Grieve* (1994), suggested:

> If we feel self-conscious or hesitant about allowing others to help us, we can recognize that their help is not only a gift to us but, to some extent, a gift to themselves as well. Shutting ourselves off from sources of help is unwise. If we say we don't need anyone, then we're closing ourselves off from others in a self-punishing and unnecessary way. Instead, we can admit how we feel, which lets others in to help us. We can reveal issues with which we are having the most difficulty. We can discuss the fact that we're not always capable, strong, logical, patient, and all those other things we need to be. (p. 116)

Think of the people in your life who care about you. When they think about your situation with your child and its impact on you, what feelings do you think they experience? It causes most people pain to see someone they love having a difficult time, especially if they feel that there is nothing they can do to make a difference in their lives. Many people feel a great sense of relief – even gratitude – when presented with something they *can* do to help.

Nancy:

My mother used to come over to the house and see the turmoil that we were in, but because of Kirsten's volatile behavior, she didn't feel comfortable offering to take care of her when she was unstable. She was always asking me if there was something she could do but I was so stressed out that I didn't even have the time to come up with something to ask her to do. Plus, I didn't want her to worry, so I always said we were fine. Finally, one day, she said, "I noticed that your heels are worn down on your black shoes. Do you want me to take them to the shoemaker for you?" At first, I gave my usual answer, that it wasn't necessary, that I could do it myself. But then I laughed and realized that I had been meaning to do it for months and just wasn't getting around to it. So, I handed her the shoes with my thanks. My shoes were finally re-soled and my mother had the satisfaction of doing something concrete that helped me.

The point is this: don't assume that providing help is a burden for the person you ask. Remember the mom whose family offered to care for her daughter who has a rare genetic disorder? She felt badly because caring for her daughter was so time-consuming. Her parents wouldn't be able to do anything else while her daughter was in their care. While she knew it in her heart, her fear of imposing on others made her miss the obvious. Her parents wanted the opportunity to love and care for their granddaughter while at the same time offering their daughter some much needed respite. Far from seeing their granddaughter as a burden, this mom's parents treasured their time with her. It was a gift to themselves as well as their daughter. As writer Ben Sweetland put it, "we cannot hold a torch to light another's path without brightening our own."

It is also helpful to remind yourself that all relationships are reciprocal. The people on your list wouldn't be actively in your life if they too were not getting something out of the relationship with you. But reciprocity doesn't necessarily mean that everything will always be "equal" in terms of who provides support at each juncture in the relationship.

One mother we spoke with elaborated on her thoughts about helping and being helped:

I felt much better about asking people for help when I stopped thinking that I had to repay each favor to the same person who helped me. I realized that there are times when I give a lot of help to other people and they may not give the same support back – but then someone else steps in and helps me when I need it. Now I try to think of it as a big circle where we help someone or someone helps us and that energy gets passed on to someone else.

Final thoughts

In this chapter, we've looked at the benefits of – and the obstacles to – building a strong support network for ourselves. Take a minute to look back through the exercises and write down the key things that you learned from this chapter.

What were your biggest revelations? What emerged as the most important things for you to focus on to build your support network?

What can you commit to doing to build your support network and your ability to ask for help? Try to write down at least five specific things you can do in the coming month. If possible, include at least one stretch "ask" – something that feels a little risky.

Mark your calendar to re-read your list in a month to see what happened. If you didn't do all of your "asks", don't be concerned. After all, it's all information! Think about what got in the way of your goals and work on your attitudes and beliefs about those areas.

It is one of the most beautiful compensations of life
that no man can sincerely try to help another
without helping himself.

Ralph Waldo Emerson, poet and essayist,
1803–1882

CHAPTER 8

Finding Personal Meaning: Unlocking the Fullness of Life

The invariable mark of wisdom is to see the
miraculous in the common.

Ralph Waldo Emerson, poet and essayist,
1803–1882

Nancy:

Finding a way to make sense of Kirsten's illness has not been easy for me. While I think of myself as a spiritual person, I couldn't reconcile my image of a loving God with that of a God that would intentionally allow a child or family to suffer as part of some greater plan. Nor did I believe that our family was somehow being tested or punished for some past behaviors or sins. And I have never found much comfort in the notion that God never gives us a burden greater than what we can bear. (How, I always wonder, do I become the type of person who can't bear any burdens and thus is handed a simple, undemanding life?).

Yet, with all my resistance to some of the more traditional religious perspectives, it has been extremely important for me to find genuine meaning in the experience of Kirsten's illness. And I have. What I've come to see is that her challenges have been a powerful catalyst for my personal growth and have the potential to become a catalyst for her growth as well.

I don't claim to fully understand the Buddhist doctrine of karma and reincarnation but there are parts of the philosophy that make sense to me as I think about Kirsten's illness and its impact on our lives. I believe that each of our lives offers us unique challenges, which we can either choose to avoid (and, the Buddhists would say, are therefore destined to repeat in another lifetime) or to embrace as an opportunity for growth and evolution.

When I look at Kirsten's illness from this perspective, I can choose to see it as an opportunity to grow and, especially, to increase my capacity for unconditional love and compassion. Having this perspective doesn't mean that I'm always able to act on these intentions – far from it! – but at least I know how I *want* to think about her illness. While I stop short of attributing intention to God in "choosing" us for Kirsten or Kirsten for us, I do know that her presence in our lives, in all its joys and challenges, has enriched us and has deepened my connection to the universe.

Deciding to write this book was also one of the ways that I chose to make personal meaning out of this experience. Meeting other families and hearing their stories has given me a much greater ability to step back from our own challenges and see them in a broader context. Their stories have inspired me and healed me in ways that I couldn't have guessed when we first began this project. Equally importantly, this book has provided an avenue for me to use my gifts for listening, synthesizing, and writing to help other people move forward with their own feelings about their children's illness or disability. That is very meaningful to me.

Do I consider Kirsten's illness to be a gift? No. Like every parent I know, my deepest wish for my child is happiness. I know enough about this illness to recognize that there is a good chance her life may be challenging and often painful. While I remain very hopeful for her future, it's still hard for me to feel anything but sadness at the prospect that the quality of her life may be diminished by having bipolar disorder. Her illness is not a gift, but *she* is a gift. I will always be grateful that we have ended up in this life together.

Linda:
When Miah was a baby I volunteered to teach Sunday school for our church's high school class. One Sunday, a young man, probably a senior in high school, said, "You know, my dad always says, it's not the cards you're dealt in this life that matters. It's what you do with them that count." This teen had a sister with Down syndrome who had died of leukemia when she was three. I felt like I had been hit over the head with a ton of bricks. I'd heard this saying before, of course, but never really *felt* its meaning. *This* was something I could hold on to. I'd been so angry in the previous months. Why had our

daughter been born with a disability? What had I done wrong? My life was never going to be the same and I wasn't happy about it! However, this sage advice meant I had something to say about the future. What was I going to do with the cards I'd been dealt? This question still guides me when making decisions about my life's direction and purpose. It has a great deal to do with why I'm involved with this book.

Viktor Frankl, a concentration camp survivor and writer, used a metaphor in his book, *Man's Search for Meaning* (1959), which describes the long term view we must have when coming to terms with the hard things that happen in our lives. He suggested we think of a movie that consists of thousands of individual frames. Each frame makes sense and has some meaning on its own, but the whole film cannot be understood until the film is seen to the end. Maybe our life is like that. We cannot know *why* until we've reached the end and maybe not even then. The ability to live with the mystery is part of the challenge and possibly a measure of our humanity. Aren't our lives' final meanings measured by how we've chosen to live (what we have done with the cards we've been dealt)? Living with grace and wisdom demands patience and a larger, longer term view.

This chapter looks at the importance of having a lens through which we view our children's illness or disability; a perspective that allows us to make sense of the situation. Finding personal meaning is different from embracing or minimizing the impacts of our children's situations. Finding personal meaning in our situation doesn't lessen the pain that we feel at times. It does, however, allow us to say with honesty "I see how to fit this experience into the larger picture of my life – and perhaps into my vision of the world beyond my own life."

The following passage was written by a mother of a six-year-old boy who lives with multiple physical disabilities causing him to be unable to walk, talk, see, or hear. This mother has found some measure of peace in this stressful situation, largely because of her own personal quest for meaning.

Since the day my son was born, I have been in a continual struggle to understand his medical complexities and long list of extensive disabilities. He has had more pain, surgeries, procedures, and other medical interventions than any other person I have met. He has endured them without the ability to communicate his pain, to ask questions, or to say no. As a family we have had to deal with chronic stress and frustrations and our activities have been greatly restricted.

I spend a lot of my energy working with the medical system's doctors, nurses, therapists, and technicians trying to get the best care for my son. More energy goes toward trying to be the best advocate for my son in the school system. Once again, administrators, principals, teachers, therapists, and aides are people I feel I need to persuade and manage. I continue to find challenges trying to get family, friends and the community to understand my son and to find an accepting place for him.

My heart is weary of asking the questions: "why my son, why all this pain, why all these disabilities?" My heart is also weary of trying to find the right doctor, therapist, or drug to "fix" him.

But sometimes now from a place of great despair in my heart, I catch a glimpse of acceptance by finding solace in nature. I visualize a magnificent mountain range and sit in awe of its beauty, power, and remoteness. Just as that mountain leaves me with emotions that I cannot express in words, I realize now that my son also has the same qualities. I sit in awe of his beauty, incredible strength to live, and ability to cope. I still struggle with frustrations and stress but now I can balance it with my new vision of my son's humanity.

This chapter comes last in the book for a reason. We have found that for many people, finding personal meaning in their child's illness or disability is something that evolves once parents have the perspective to look at their situation over time. For many of us, the road to finding personal meaning begins with a pronounced *lack* of ability to find personal meaning.

Nancy:
John and I went through many years of infertility treatment before adopting Kirsten and Molly. I had a friend who was going through a similar process at the same time and she was very angry. She would ask "Why me? There are all these terrible parents in the world who don't even want their children. Why are we struggling with this? It's so unfair." I had no answer for her. I also thought it was unfair but somehow I never went to "Why me." Instead I thought "Why not me? It's got to happen to someone and I've been pretty lucky in my life so far. This is just our thing that we'll have to deal with." It was a difficult period in our lives but I never despaired. I knew that I would be a parent one day.

> I felt pretty good about my ability to handle adversity – at least in this particular situation. But my positive attitude disappeared when Kirsten's illness began to take hold. All my latent "Why me" energy suddenly kicked into gear and I too was consumed by the unfairness of it all. I had new empathy for how my friend felt. I couldn't make sense of why this was happening to Kirsten and to us. I only knew that I felt miserable.

In the initial shock of dealing with our child's illness or disability, many parents are unable to detach enough to even consider how this experience will ultimately fit into their world view or the broader course of their lives. They are fully consumed with getting through the immediate challenges and dealing with the onslaught of raw and painful feelings.

The Dalai Lama presents a Buddhist perspective on finding meaning in the midst of pain in his book, *The Art of Happiness* (1998). He advises us to be gentle with ourselves in the midst of crisis and notes that even the most resilient person is likely to have difficulty focusing on their beliefs – no matter how positive they may be – about the meaning of their suffering in the midst of the storm. He writes:

> Finding meaning in suffering is a powerful method of helping us cope even during the most trying times in our lives. But finding meaning in our suffering is not an easy task ... During periods of acute crisis and tragedy, it seems impossible to reflect on any possible meaning behind our suffering. And it's natural to view our suffering as senseless and unfair, and wonder, "Why me?" (p. 199)

However, he goes on to point out the importance of finding personal meaning once the flood of feelings has subsided.

> Fortunately during times of comparative ease, periods before or after acute experiences of suffering, we can reflect on suffering, seeking to develop an understanding of its meaning. And the time and effort we spend searching for meaning in suffering will pay great rewards when bad things begin to strike. But in order to reap those rewards, we must begin our search for meaning when things are going well. A tree with strong roots can withstand the most violent storm, but the tree can't grow roots just as the storm appears on the horizon. (p. 200)

We liken the Dalai Lama's comments to the famous Hierarchy of Needs model developed by Abraham Maslow in the late 1960s. This hierarchy, represented in the shape of a pyramid, theorizes that people's needs change as their life circumstances change. At the lower levels of the pyramid, the needs relate to safety, food and shelter, but, at the higher levels, needs change to social interaction and self-worth culminating at the highest level with self-actualization. For example, Maslow would argue, it is difficult for someone who is starving to focus on whether his or her need for self-expression is being satisfied.

Norman Kunc (1998), a educator and researcher in the field of special education, has developed an analogous pyramid for parents of children with special needs. At the bottom is the need to simply survive. Once the acute crisis has passed, however, many of us try our best to move up the pyramid and towards "higher level" states of acceptance and adjustment. We have met some rare individuals who are able to immediately accept the situation. Most of us, however, have trouble skipping steps. It's hard to focus on the upper echelon of the pyramid if we are still struggling with survival, resources, belonging and acceptance.

Obtaining support and resources generally comes before acceptance. We usually cannot move to full acceptance of our child's differences before we have a created a community of belonging and acceptance for our child and ourselves. We need a safe place to speak our feelings of frustration and resentment. This is normal and helpful. We have found that when families have this outlet, the acceptance comes. It is important to realize that it is not an all or nothing event. Our own experience says that acceptance comes in little pieces and ebbs and flows.

Usually our early feelings contain some aspect of grief or loss. In her book, *Ambiguous Loss: Learning to Live with Unresolved Grief* (1999), Pauline Boss defines ambiguous loss as types of losses that are fundamentally open-ended such as chronic illness or disability or a missing child or spouse. She points out that the grieving process in these situations has many similarities to the grief that follows a death but with the important difference that the loss lacks finality.

This makes grieving the loss particularly challenging. In her research, Boss found that the most successful survivors of ambiguous losses are those people who can make meaning out of the situation. She notes the following:

The last and most difficult step in resolving any loss is to make sense of it. In the case of ambiguous loss, gaining meaning is even more difficult than in an ordinary loss, because grief itself remains unresolved. But if we cannot make sense out of ambiguity, nothing really changes. We merely endure.

The goal for families is to find some way to change even though the ambiguity remains. This is yet another paradox – to transform a situation that won't change.

Many people succeed… It is not the situation that changes but what they hope for. When an illness won't go away, people creatively find hope in other ways – in doing their best to manage the illness, in helping others who are experiencing the same pain, or in finding ways to prevent others from having the same experience. With surprising ingenuity, people infuse what looks like a tragic situation with hope. (p. 119)

Boss found several factors that impact an individual's ability to find meaning from ambiguous loss, including family of origin and early social experience, spiritual beliefs, and basic personality orientation towards optimism or pessimism.

An interesting finding of her research was that the "it's not fair" perspective can actually be very helpful to people who are grieving ambiguous losses. She notes that the ability to live with uncertainty and to accept that the world is often random and unfair is, in fact, often a hallmark of people who are able to make meaning of their ambiguous loss. These people are willing to concede that we can't always know why things happen but avoid blaming themselves for their situation. By contrast, those who see the world as fair – a world where we reap the rewards and punishments of our own making – may be overwhelmed by the belief that they somehow deserved their loss and unable to move on.

In his book, *When Bad Things Happen to Good People* (2004), Harold Kushner shares his belief that our *reaction* to pain rather than the pain itself defines the person we become. He comments:

Pain is the price we pay for being alive… When we understand that, our question will change from, "Why do we have to feel pain?" to "what do we do with our pain so that it becomes meaningful and not just pointless empty suffering? How can we turn all the painful experiences of our lives into birth pangs or into growing pains?" We may not ever understand why we suffer or be able to control the forces that cause our suffering, but we can have a lot to say about what suffering does to us, and what sort of people we become because of it. Pain makes some people bitter and envious. It makes others sensitive and compassionate. It is the result, not the cause, of pain that makes some experiences of pain meaningful and others empty and destructive. (p. 64)

In *Contentment: A Way to True Happiness* (1999), Robert A. Johnson and Jerry M. Ruhl talk about the importance of acknowledging our constant battle with opposing points of view. We may feel anxious and worried because we see contradiction in our lives. This can grind our contentment to bits. We want to lose weight, but also want to eat that chocolate bar. Which do we choose? In reality, we need both sides to know contentment. Without suffering, we would not know joy. When we can honor both sides of our feelings, we are more aligned with "what is" instead of our own projections about reality.

Linda:

I am at a point in my own work around my daughter's disability where I am dealing with feeling two emotions at once – pride in all her accomplishments and sorrow at times for things she finds difficult. In an ordinary day, I'm sometimes aware of my opposing points of view. I feel happy and grateful that she has some really great friends and sad that she doesn't have a close friend at school. Time and my own contemplation of this situation have helped me realize I can embrace both of these feelings. If I can allow myself to feel my pain about the school situation, I can feel more joy about the fact that she does have some really great friends in other venues. This helps me see what truly is and things feel honest. It helps me see what I need to do next. For instance, Miah has friends at school but none are particularly close. Who might that one good friend be? Who should we invite over? I have found if I do this and ask myself what the next "what is true?" is, I am led to the next right thing.

On these days when I can look at each circumstance honestly, acknowledging the good and bad, I find I'm much more relaxed and content. Being honest and present with my own feelings, neither avoiding nor seeing the world through rose colored glasses, helps me create what I feel is truthful about my daughter's situation, and thus, I actually feel more joyful on those days.

One mother we interviewed wrote this about how she makes meaning of her daughter's very challenging situation of seizures, cerebral palsy, and developmental disabilities.

> As I raise my daughter, I am often aware of holding two emotions at once. They can seem to be incompatible, like fear and hope, but being consciously aware of this duality is like a yogic pose that helps me find my center. It is a recognition of the balance that life is, because it is forgiving and allows for paradox. It simplifies by making room for complexity and joy to co-exist. I know that at the very least, I am fully living.

We were fascinated at the diversity of answers we received when talking with parents about how they made meaning of their child's needs. We'd like to share some of the thoughts of parents as they described their individual ways of making meaning. Please notice how no answer is more *right* than another.

This mother, who has a daughter with Down syndrome, found her meaning in the form of the many people who have entered her life because of her daughter.

> We go to church but I wouldn't say that we're religious in the sense that I think, "Oh, God gave us this little gift". But I do think that nothing is coincidental. I think Stacy came to us for a reason, not necessarily a religious reason. I think of all the people we've met because of Stacy that we'd never met before. Some incredible, incredible people have come into our lives and I would like to believe that Stacy was the catalyst for it. Everyone has to come to a way to make their situation feel like it's OK, to be able to say "this is what it is and this is what we have". It's just so different for everybody. Yes, I definitely think there was a reason. Will I ever know the reason why? Probably not, but there are so many things that have happened because of Stacy, it's been pretty neat.

A father of a child with Down syndrome found that the values of his parents and grandparents gave him a framework for viewing his son's disability in a positive way.

> Growing up, my grandmother was a midwife. My mother would tell me all of the stories about difficult births and children with different kinds of needs. She would say, "This child is what God has given you and you treat them like anyone else in the family. You don't exclude

them, and they are part of the family." I think it is that attitude I grew up with, which is important to us in how we treat Ramon.

Sometimes personal meaning is played out through our career direction or objectives. The experience of dealing with her son's developmental delays gave this mom a new perspective on where she wanted to go with her work.

I've never really gone through a long period of grieving and depression about Josh's disability. He was pregnancy #8 [after a series of miscarriages] so he was just an incredible gift. I also felt that there was a reason why he was here. I was going to nursing school and I was going into midwifery. But when Josh came along, I saw that the gulf between medical community and the outside community is huge – especially when you have a child that has medical issues. They really don't care about therapy or the whole child beyond the medical issue – there's no connection. So it's focused my energy on learning to be a connection for people. So that's where I'm heading with my nursing. I'm not really "New Agey". In general, I don't really buy into that but somehow with Josh I do. I feel like we're all kind of learning from him.

This mom found her meaning in the process of parenting itself – a role that has tremendous meaning to her – and her faith in God.

I have come to the place where the meaning is that I am raising a daughter. Every child has issues and this happens to be hers. I gained some confidence going through all of the process of medical stuff because I was good at navigating the system. She is different and I think that we are doing a good job with that. Knowing that there is someone greater than me that loves me and has a plan that is bigger than me is helpful. God already knows what is going to happen and he is watching out for me.

Linda:

I get strength from my spiritual beliefs. I believe we make our own meaning. I like to think that God is present in all situations, and that the trick is finding God within ourselves and others. I believe God weeps when we weep and rejoices when we rejoice. And I think that seeing Miah as having God within has been very helpful to me. I believe she is loved just as she is and is all she needs to be. If I look at her with my spiritual belief glasses and not my ego belief glasses that sometimes need to fix, I'm much more at peace and a much better mother. I want to honor her as "perfect" just as she is, and help her see herself as a lovely, wonderful girl. Through offering resources, support, and lots of rich experiences I believe I can help her much more than when I try to change her. I don't believe God "chose" my family to have a child with special needs. I do believe that God is with my family and daughter at all times. My task is to experience God's love for us all. I know a lot of families do believe a Higher Power preordained everything and they find comfort in this. As long as we all make sense of our situation in a way that feels true to us, we're on the path to more peace in our daily lives.

These quotes are all from parents who have had the opportunity to reflect on the personal meaning of their child's illness or disability. But how do you create personal meaning in this situation if it is not already there? One way to start is by talking to parents whom you respect about their journey and how they have made meaning of their child's difference.

We believe that finding personal meaning is not something that can be forced or scheduled into your life. Sometimes we need some distance before things become clear.

There is no right or wrong approach to the challenge of finding personal meaning. But finding *some* level of meaning in the situation was a hallmark for the truly happy parents that we met along the way. Parker J. Palmer (1990), a Quaker theologian, wrote:

Real despair comes from clinging to the conviction that if I cannot "make meaning" for my life – by making money, friends, changes – there is no meaning to life at all. True despair is the refusal to recognize the fragility of all our efforts at making [meaning], the ease with which our making is destroyed by error, evil, illness, age, death. The joy beyond despair comes when we abandon the exhausting illusion of self-sufficiency and become the grateful recipients of the gifts that life provides. (p. 83)

However, we have noticed that the personal meanings people find in their children's challenges tend to be very congruent with the way they think about their values and most deeply held beliefs. Therefore, we believe that examining our core values and beliefs is an important step in creating a personal framework for our child's situation that can support and sustain us.

Exercise 8.1: Articulating your personal values

In this exercise, we are going to focus on articulating our personal values so that we can look at them as a framework for articulating the personal meaning we find in our children's situations.

1. Think about someone you admire. What is it about that person that you admire?

2. What qualities are most important to you in other people?

3. What qualities do you value most in yourself? Describe a time when you felt that you made an important contribution to your family, your community or to the world.

4. If your biggest fan was describing you to another person, what would they say about why you are so wonderful?

Exercise 8.2: Personal meaning and your parenting experience

1. Thinking about all your answers from the previous exercise. How have your personal values shaped the way you have approached parenting your child?

2. Everyone's experience of finding personal meaning is different. How would you describe the personal meaning you have found in the experience of raising a child with special needs? If you have any trouble answering this question, thinking about your answers to the following questions may be helpful:

   • How has parenting your child changed or deepened your connection to your spiritual practices or beliefs?

   • How has it changed your interactions with other people?

   • How has it changed your parenting style with your other children?

- How has it impacted your career or your feeling about your career?

- How has it changed your priorities or your sense of what is important in life?

- How have you changed or evolved as a result of parenting your child?

While everyone comes to meaning in their own way and time, we have found that certain attitudes and practices can be helpful in cultivating these feelings. Attaining happiness and meaning are such important topics that hundreds, perhaps thousands, of books have been written on this topic. While we have read only a small sampling of these books, we have found that a handful of concepts emerge time and time again as the cornerstone of building a meaningful life. These concepts include awareness, gratitude, and giving back to others. Developing regular practices that focus us on these attributes help to create an internal state of mind where it becomes possible to find meaning and joy.

Awareness

Awareness goes by many other names including attention, noticing, and being present. Whatever the term, awareness speaks of intention. It implies a decision to live consciously if only for a moment, to turn off our "auto pilot" mode and really look at what is all around us.

Nancy:

Last winter I was finishing up several months of heavy travel. I landed in San Diego feeling tired and grumpy and walked off the plane into an obviously new terminal building. Since I spend a lot of time in airports and love interior design, I pay close attention to airports. My first reaction on looking at the terminal was to think "What a bland terminal. They spent all this money building a new terminal and it has absolutely nothing interesting or visually pleasing about it". Then, totally out of the blue, I decided to challenge myself to find ten things I liked about the terminal. Suddenly I began to see the cool lighting fixtures, an interesting pattern in the rug, even a nicely designed water fountain. I had gotten up to nine things I liked just as I was approaching the escalator bank that led down to baggage. In my experience, baggage areas are low probability places to find beauty so I was looking hard for #10 before I got on the escalator. As I came around the corner, half hidden on the wall behind the escalators were two spectacularly beautiful paintings. I literally dropped my briefcase and just stood there admiring them for about five minutes. Then I began to watch other people passing by and realized that hardly a soul even glanced at these amazing works of art as they hurried to get their bags. And there is no doubt in my mind that I would have missed them too had I not been looking for #10. After that experience, I began to play the "10 things" game with myself at times when I feel bored, grumpy or stale. Sometimes I look for 10 things I've never noticed before on my way to driving the kids to school. Sometimes I try to find 10 things that I think are funny. Whatever my "challenge du jour", this little game reminds me to be conscious and present; to really *see* what I am seeing. Usually it lifts my mood and reminds me that there are amazing things all around me if I take the time to look.

Linda:

Years ago, I had the great privilege of traveling throughout China, Pakistan and India with my husband. I began to notice that some days I was quite happy and other days I was easily bothered or discontent. I noticed that it was not my present surroundings that influenced my mood as much as my *attitude*. I learned that for me, everything is a function of attitude. I try to remember this, but it is a hard lesson to truly live. And I've also learned that for me, my attitude is greatly affected by how *awake* I am. I find that participating in activities that help me feel alive, *awaken* me. I feel less numb to my surroundings. For instance, when I engage in activities where I lose myself, where time seems to float away, where I feel calm and present, the rest of my life feels much more in sync. I take the hard things in my stride. When I dance, or hike, or journal, or laugh with a friend, I find it much easier to enjoy the sometimes difficult moments of my day: getting my daughters off to school, having a conversation with Miah where I'm not understanding her, or helping with homework. My attitude predicts the success of these experiences much more than these experiences affect my attitude. If I'm not diligent about keeping my attitude in right focus, I can feel dull, disconnected, and numb to my life. My day seems wasted when I live in a fog or frenzy. To me, having a positive feeling about my life is directly related to listening to my inner voice and making sure my needs are being met as best they can be. Then I can tune into the present with strength, courage, and a knowing that I'm living fully.

Exercise 8.3: Focusing on awareness

Remember that mindfulness, being purely present in the moment, is always as close as your next breath. Anytime we stop, look at our surroundings – the picture on the wall or the tree out our window – we are more present. You might practice stopping what you are doing, looking at what is around you, listening to the sounds near by, smelling the air or your perfume, touching your skin, and even tasting the inside of your mouth. Notice your breathing. Whenever we tune into our senses, we become more present and in the moment. This little practice can be of tremendous help when you are feeling anxious. Practice it often and when you are feeling unsettled and you can quickly experience a better sense of calm.

As you are paying attention to your day, think about the following:

1. What did I eat today? Did I take the time to sit down and enjoy the food or did I eat it on the run? What could I eat that I would really relish? (Try to pick something healthy but an occasional treat is a good thing too!)

2. How did my body feel when I woke up this morning? Did I feel rested? Did anything feel uncomfortable?

3. How was I feeling about my child(ren) today? Did I take the time to notice the cute or funny thing that happened?

Gratitude

It is a short step from awareness to gratitude. Once we put our awareness on finding things that feel positive or hopeful, it becomes much easier to find things for which we are grateful.

Nancy:
Several years ago, John and I were raking leaves in our backyard. It was what a friend of mine calls a "Chamber of Commerce" day: sunny, crisp, boundless blue skies. Kirsten was having a great day and was playing happily with a friend, running around and laughing. Her face

looked relaxed and calm. Molly, toddling after the big girls, was also having a wonderful time. We spent the afternoon raking and bagging our leaves, stopping to enjoy the sight of our beautiful children playing in the sun. Late that afternoon another friend dropped by. "What have you been up to today?" she asked. I pointed to the bags of leaves and said "Pretty much this." She made a face and commented "That doesn't look like much fun." I looked at her and said in all seriousness, "This has been the best day of my life."

I've thought about that moment many times since that day. I've wondered if I exaggerated for the sake of drama. What about my wedding day, our kids' adoption days, and the many other "big" events of my life? But even as I considered other happy days, that day spent raking leaves continued to stand out as one of the best days I had ever had. A day of pure pleasure without the burden of expectation and tension that so often accompany our more momentous days. I experienced what it meant to be in the moment and to fully appreciate the perfection of everyday life. It made me wonder how many other perfect days I had taken for granted over the course of my life.

I can see now that this simple, sunny, leaf-raking day was really the first time I ever had an inkling of what people meant when they talked about having sorrow and joy in equal measure. I saw that my capacity to appreciate life had been heightened and sharpened in ways that I never anticipated. What an unexpected gift. And I was deeply grateful, not just for the beauty of the day but also for my newfound ability to see life as a miracle, to rejoice in the sheer wonder of a pile of bagged leaves, a sunny day, and a happy child.

Linda:
A few years ago I read the book, *Simple Abundance: A Daybook of Comfort and Joy* by Sarah Ban Breathnach (1995), and I found my life changing simply by following one of her six principles of abundant living: Gratitude. I began to write three things per day that I was thankful for. When I started noticing all that I had, I felt rich and blessed indeed. I noticed that it was the little things that gave me the most joy. These were the essentials of truly living well. That kiss from my daughter, the little pat and wink from my husband, or the kind words from a friend. By tapping into the power of gratitude, I felt more excitement for my life more frequently. I smiled more. I've

quit writing my three gratitude sentences a day, but after writing this paragraph, you can bet I'm going back to it.

Exercise 8.4: Cultivating a sense of gratitude

For the next week, take five minutes before you go to sleep and jot down three things that happened that day for which you feel grateful. It is a wonderful tool for helping us rediscover our joy. Make a list of anything that makes you laugh, smile, and feel happy. Don't forget the small stuff.

Day 1:

Day 2:

Day 3:

Day 4:

Day 5:

Day 6:

Day 7:

Giving back to others

The desire to give back to others is frequently a natural outgrowth of finding personal meaning in our children's experiences.

Often we hear a calling to use our gifts to help those in need. We sense we can not help all situations. It is quite natural for our focus to be on helping others in similar circumstances to our own. This is perhaps why many of us choose to spend our time, resources, and gifts helping families with children with special needs. Others of us may want to help in an area that is not connected to our current situation at all.

What is important to remember is that when we are able to step out of our own situation and focus on another, we feel better too. The key here is the phrase, "when we are able." If we are in crisis, or our situation is fresh, putting our energy outside ourselves and our families may not be appropriate. Sometimes helping our children is all we can do. But when the time is right, using our gifts to create a better world goes a long way in helping create our *own* happier, more joyful life.

Giving back to others takes many different forms. Sometimes it is very small and personal. One mother shared how she makes a point of catching the eye of a parent who is struggling with an out-of-control child in a public place and giving a supportive smile or comment that lets the parent know that he or she is not alone and that others understand and sympathize.

Participating in support groups – whether face to face or through an online list-serv – is also a tremendous way that parents give back to others by sharing wisdom, experience and support.

Other parents find that getting involved in more systematic changes is where their passion and talents lie. One mother whose daughter has a variety of physical and cognitive challenges shared the following:

> Whenever I am faced with a situation where I need to advocate for my daughter, I try to make the micro macro. So, rather than just think about what I can do to help my daughter, I also think about how making changes to the situation could benefit other children. For example, when my daughter was in fifth grade, her class was going on an off-site picnic to celebrate the end of the school year. I signed the permission slip and didn't give it another thought. The morning of the field trip, I got a call asking me how Hannah was going to be transported to the picnic. I said that I assumed that she would be going with the other kids on the bus. I was informed that this was not going to be acceptable and that she would have to miss the picnic unless I could transport her myself. After much discussion about liability issues and such, we finally found an acceptable compromise and Hannah was able to go to the picnic.
>
> Once the event was over, however, I went to the school and helped them re-draft the field permission form to add a box asking if the child had any special transportation needs and if these needs had been addressed by the school or the parents. This alerted both parents and teachers to the fact that transportation for kids with special needs had to be thought through well ahead of time and, hopefully, avoided the last minute fire drill that we went through. I always try to look for ways to leverage what I do for Hannah to help other kids in the same situation.

Still other parents become involved in state and federal policy, assuming key roles in lobbying for change in programs, legislation, and funding. Whether we help one person or help to make changes that impact many, it is important to realize that there are no lesser gifts. Each is crucial to contributing to the diversity of all the needs of our hurting world.

Exercise 8.5: Knowing our gifts

Giving back to others is most satisfying when it taps into our own unique gifts and strengths. Thinking back over your life, list some of the ways that you have been helpful to other people. (Don't forget things that might have been "small" to you, but helped someone else.)

1. Which of these acts of giving was the most personally satisfying to you?

2. Do you see any patterns in your list? Do you gravitate towards the personal or the systematic? What just feels right and gives you pleasure when you're engaged with it?

3. If the time was right for you and your family, what types of involvement would "call to you" in terms of giving back to others?

Final thoughts

Congratulations! You've made it through the entire book. You are well on your way to living a joyful life.

Take a few minutes to reflect on your journey and ask yourself the following questions:

- Am I clear on what I want for myself?

- Have I made myself a priority in my own life?

- Do I give myself permission to fully experience my feelings?

- How have I changed and grown because of my child?

- Am I able to break out of negative thought patterns and move to a more useful perspective?

- Am I satisfied with the community I have built for myself and for my child?

- Am I moving through my life with intention and consciousness, acknowledging and appreciating the good as well as the challenging?

- What unique gifts can I offer the world?

Come back to this page every six months or so and reflect on your answers. Go back and re-do some of the exercises. (We do this with some regularity.)

Nancy:
Occasionally as Linda and I have worked on this book, I have hit a low point and have exclaimed to my husband or a friend, "Look at me! I'm a mess. Who am *I* to be giving advice to other people on living a joyful life."

Yes, I'm sorry to say that thinking deeply about this issue for the past two years and writing a book on the topic has not made my life perfect. I still have terrible days when I want to run away. I have days, even weeks, when I still succumb to negative thinking. I have times when I forget to take care of myself and I hole up at home neglecting the community that I have carefully built.

So, what's different? First, the bad times are shorter and less frequent. Instead of settling in for several months of misery, I can say "Oh well. This is a bad day, week, etc. It won't last forever." I have confidence that I will be able to reclaim my sense of equilibrium. I can also look at my life over the past several years and see what I have been able to accomplish. From planting a perennial garden to starting a new business, I can see how much my energy and enthusiasm has returned even if it isn't there every single day. In the spirit of gratitude, what else can I ask for?

Linda:

When I think about the past 12 years of my life, I realize the journey I'm on now didn't start the day Miah was born, but the day I decided to think about and act on her disability in a different way. I realize now that my journey has been comprised of baby steps all the way, but the further I go, the more of my days feel like they are sprinkled with fulfillment and joy. This is a process, not an arrival – and I'm actually glad about that.

As I moved along, I found that, without even realizing it, Miah's diagnosis was no longer constantly on my mind. When I started believing in her and my creativity, wisdom, and purpose for this life, I started really living again. In fact, I'm thinking and doing things I never thought possible! This evolution has had many sources – but one of the most important has been doing the exercises in this workbook.

Some of you may have done all of them already and are feeling better, some may have done them and are waiting for these principles, tools, and strategies to take root in your life, while others of you may be reading bits and pieces of the book, but haven't actually done any of the exercises. Still others are reading the last page first. Believe Nancy and me, *doing the work*, actually picking up a pebble and throwing it into the water, will pay off for you. The exercises, or pebbles, will send tiny ripples of movement forward in your life, and you will feel differently.

So treat yourself kindly. Trust the process. Find some quiet moments for contemplation. Soon you'll find things don't hurt quite as much anymore. If you've lost your enthusiasm for life, it will return. And if you find it's taking longer than you would like, reach out to others. In the words of Ivy Baker Priest (1958, p. 78), "the world is round and the place which may seem like the end may also be only the beginning."

The Earth is crammed with Heaven.

Elizabeth Barrett Browning, poet, 1806–1861

Additional Resources

There are many books, videos, magazines, websites, and organizations that provide a myriad of information for families about their children with special needs. Since this information is already available online we will not try to replicate it here, but point you to some fine websites where you can create your own resource guide.

The National Information Center for Children and Youth with Disabilities, at www.nichcy.org, is an exceptional national information center. It focuses on children and youth, from birth to age 22.

TASH at http://www.tash.org, is an international association of people with disabilities, and their families, advocates, teachers and professionals working toward inclusion in all areas of life. They also put on a wonderful annual conference.

Each state also has its own parent training and information center (PTI). These organizations are run for and by parents of children with differences reaching out to assist families and professionals. You can find your PTI by going to www.taalliance.org/PTIs.htm.

Each mental illness and disability label has its own organization that provides information and support. The Internet can be a wonderful resource for accessing these organizations.

As we have commented in this book, reading has been an inspiring guide for our own work towards healing. The titles below either come from our own bookshelves or from ones we trust. Many of them are classics in self-help literature. We've organized these suggestions by chapter title though many could easily be paired with other chapters. These lists are in no way exhaustive. Please add your own favorites and email us at info@shiftingview.com with your suggestions.

Chapter 2: Putting On Your Oxygen Mask: Intention and Self-care

Martha Beck, *Finding Your Own North Star: How to Claim the Life You Were Meant to Live*, New York: Three Rivers Press, 2002.

Susan Jeffers, *Feel the Fear and Do It Anyway*, New York: Ballantine Books, 1988.

Chapter 3: The Twisted Skein: Embracing Our Complex and Conflicting Feelings

These titles are about the bigger picture – approaching our lives with depth and perspective.

William Bridges, *Transitions: Making Sense of Life's Changes*, New York: Perseus Books, 1980.

Nancy B. Miller, *Nobody's Perfect: Living and Growing with Children Who Have Special Needs*, Baltimore, MD: Brookes Publishing Co., 2002.

M. Scott Peck, *The Road Less Traveled*, New York: Touchstone, 2003.

Tom Sullivan, *Special Parent, Special Child: Parents of Children with Disabilities Share Their Trials, Triumphs and Hard-Won Wisdom*. New York: Putnam, 1996.

Chapter 4: Seeing With New Eyes: Reframing Our Perceptions and Beliefs

These books aren't necessarily on reframing, but all are about the power of thought and you can change your experience by changing your thoughts.

Richard Carlson, *What About the BIG stuff? Finding Strength and Moving Forward When the Stakes are High*, New York: Hyperion, 2002.

Albert Ellis, *A Guide to Rational Living*, Chatsworth, CA: Wilshire Book Company, 1966.

Louise Hay, *You Can Heal Your Life*, Carlsbad, CA: Hay House, Inc., 1999.

Ellen Langer, *Mindfulness: Choice and Control in Everyday Life*, New York: Perseus Books, 1989.

Phillip McGraw, *Life Strategies: Doing What Works, Doing What Matters*, New York: Hyperion, 1999.

Chapter 5: Shrinking the Balloon: Seeing Our Child as a Whole Person

Martha Beck, *Expecting Adam*, New York: Berkley Books, 1999.

J. Lindemann and S. Lindemann, *Growing Up Proud: A Parent's Guide to the Psychological Care of Children with Disabilities*, Clayton: Warner Books, 1988.

William Martin, *The Parents' Tao Te Ching*, New York: Marlowe and Company, 1999.

Chapter 6: Building Our Children's Village: Deepening Our Child's Connection to Others

These titles are either about our kids or will help us become better advocates for our children.

Stephen Covey, *The 7 Habits of Highly Effective People*, New York: Simon and Schuster, Inc., 1989.

Nicholas Martin, *A Guide to Collaboration for IEP Teams*, Baltimore, MD: Brookes Publishing Co., 2005.

Debbie Staub, *Delicate Threads: Friendships Between Children with and without Special Needs in Inclusive Settings*, Bethesda, MD: Woodbine House, 1998.

Linda J. Stengle, *Laying Community Foundations for Your Child with a Disability: How to Establish Relationships That Will Support Your Child after You're Gone*, Bethesda, MD: Woodbine House, 1996.

Beret Strong and John Tweedy, *Song of Our Children*, Boulder, CO: Landlocked Films, 2005.
This is a wonderful film about inclusion for school-aged children.

Chapter 7: Knocking on the Door: Creating Our Personal Support Systems

Carolyn R. Shaffer and Kristin Anundsen, *Creating Community Anywhere*, New York: Penguin Putnam, Inc., 1993.

Marla Paul, *The Friendship Crisis: Finding, Making, and Keeping Friends When You're Not a Kid Anymore*, New York: Rodale Press, 2005.

References

Ban Breathnach, S. (1995) *Simple Abundance: A Daybook of Comfort and Joy.* New York: Warner Books.

Baker Priest, I. (1958) *The Green Grows Ivy.* New York: McGraw-Hill.

Boss, P. (1999) *Ambiguous Loss: Learning to Live with Unresolved Grief.* Massachusetts: Harvard University Press.

Burns, D. (1999) *The Feeling Good Handbook.* New York: Penguin Putman.

Cameron, J. (1996) *The Artist's Way: A Spiritual Path to Higher Creativity.* New York: Penguin Putman Press.

Choquette, S. (1997) *Your Heart's Desire: Instructions for Creating the Life You Really Want.* New York: Three River Press.

Clinton, H. Rodham (1996) *It Takes a Village: And Other Lessons Children Teach Us.* New York: Touchstone.

Dalai Lama and Cutler, H. (1998) *The Art of Happiness: A Handbook for Living.* New York: Penguin.

Early, T. and Gregoire, T. (2002) 'Child Functioning and Caregiver Well-Being in Families of Children with Emotional Disorders: A Longitudinal Analysis.' *Journal of Family Issues 23,* 392–409.

Foster, R. and Hicks, G. (2004) *How We Choose to Be Happy: The Nine Choices of Extremely Happy People – Their Secrets and Their Stories.* New York: Berkley Publishing Group.

Frankl, V. (1959) *Man's Search for Meaning.* New York: Buccaneer Books.

Gibran, K. (1978) *The Prophet.* New York: Alfred A. Knopf.

Healey, W. (1996) 'Helping Parents Deal with the Fact Their Child has a Disability.' *Council for Exceptional Children 3,* 5, November. Online at www.ldonline.org/articles/5937.

Johnson, R. and Ruhl, J. (1999) *Contentment: A Way to True Happiness.* New York: Harper Collins.

Klein, S. and Schive, K. (eds) (2001) *You Will Dream New Dreams: Inspiring Personal Stories by Parents of Children with Disabilities.* New York: Kensington Publishing Corporation.

Kunc, N. (1998) *The Need to Belong: Rediscovering Maslow's Hierarchy of Needs.* Nanaimo, BC: Axis Consultation and Training.

Kushner, H. (2004) *When Bad Things Happen to Good People.* New York: Harper Collins.

Louden, J. (1992) *The Woman's Comfort Book: A Self-Nurturing Guide for Restoring Balance in Your Life.* New York: Harper Collins.

Mansfield, K. (1927) *Journal of Katherine Mansfield.* New York: Alfred A. Knopf.

McAnaney, K. (1998) *I Wish...: Dreams and Realities of Parenting a Special Needs Child.* Santa Barbara, CA: Special Needs Project.

Miller, D. (2003) *Your Surviving Spirit: A Spiritual Workbook for Coping with Trauma.* Oakland, CA: New Harbinger Publications.

Miller, N. (2002) *Nobody's Perfect: Living and Growing with Children Who Have Special Needs.* Baltimore, MD: Brookes Publishing Co.

Moore, T. (1992) *Care of the Soul: A Guide for Cultivating Depth and Sacredness in Everyday Life.* New York: Harper Collins.

Palmer, P. (1999) *Let Your Life Speak: Listening for the Voice of Vocation.* San Francisco: Jossey-Bass.

Rosenberg, J. (1985) *Body, Self, and Soul: Sustaining Integration.* Atlanta, GA: Humanics Ltd.

Seligman, M. and Darling, R. (1997) *Ordinary Families, Special Children: A Systems Approach to Childhood Disability.* New York: Guilford Publications.

Siebert, A. (1996) *The Survivor Personality.* New York: Berkley Publishing Group.

Staudacher, C. (1994) *A Time to Grieve: Mediations for Healing After the Death of a Loved One.* New York: Harper Collins.

Stewart, A. (2003) 'Metamorphosis'. Unpublished poem.

Sullivan, T. (1996) *Special Parent, Special Child.* New York: Tarcher.

Turnbull, A. and Turnbull, R. (2001) *Families, Professionals, and Exceptionality: Collaborating for Empowerment.* New Jersey: Prentice Hall.

Ungar, M. (ed.) (2005) *Handbook for Working with Children and Youth: Pathways to Resilience across Cultures and Contexts.* Thousand Oaks, CA: Sage Publications.

Wolin, S.J. and Wolin, S. (1999) 'Project Resilience Core Concepts.' Online at: www.projectresilience.com/framesconcepts.htm.

Wright, J. (2003) *There Must Be More Than This.* New York: Random House, Inc.

Index